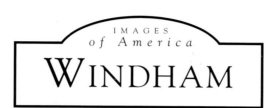

IMAGES
of America

WINDHAM

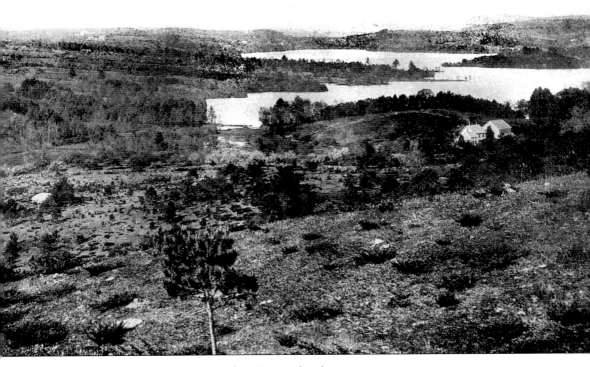

Andover's steeples there were seen,
While o'er the vast expanse between,
I did with wonder gaze;
There, as it were beneath my feet,
I view'd my father's pleasant seat—
My joy in younger days.
There Windham Range, in flowery vest,
Was seen in robes of green,
While Cobbet's Pond, from east to west,
Spread her bright waves between.
Cows lowing, cocks crowing,
While frogs on Cobbet's shore,
Lay croaking and mocking,
The bull's tremendous roar.

—From "Farewell to the Muses,"
by Robert Dinsmoor, "the Rustic Bard,"
Windham, February 26, 1811

On the cover: The Albert Campbell farm is pictured on the cover of this volume. (Baldwin Coolidge No. 154-B; courtesy of SPNEA.)

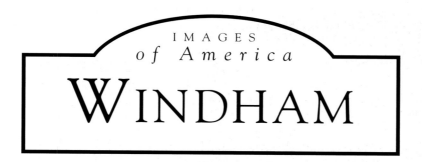

IMAGES
of America

WINDHAM

Bradford R. Dinsmore

ARCADIA

First published 2003
Reprinted 2004

Published by Arcadia Publishing,
Charleston SC, Chicago IL, Portsmouth NH, San Francisco CA

Printed in Great Britain

Library of Congress Catalog Card Number: 2003107809

For all general information, contact Arcadia Publishing:
Telephone 843-853-2070
Fax 843-853-0044
E-mail sales@arcadiapublishing.com
For customer service and orders:
Toll-free 1-888-313-2665

Visit us on the Internet at www.arcadiapublishing.com

*Dedicated to my sons Matthew and Isaac Dinsmore
and to the future generations of Windham.*

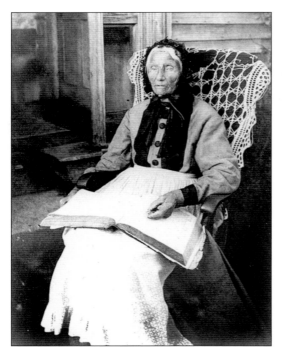

This noble matriarch of Windham, with her family Bible sitting on her lap, is Sally Clark. She was the daughter of John Campbell and was born in 1794. She married John Carr and lived on the Carr homestead near her home. After her first husband died, she married Calvin Clark. She was 91 years of age when she died in 1885 and was Windham's oldest resident at the time. She was beloved by the people of both Windham and Londonderry who knew her simply as Aunt Sally. In his column in the *Exeter Newsletter,* William S. Harris wrote, "She was a good 'mother of Israel,' who was eminently active and helpful in her life, full of good works and alms' deeds which she did willingly, and she had the respect and love of all." This photograph was taken prior to 1885 in her doorway, where she often greeted her neighbors and friends.

CONTENTS

ACKNOWLEDGMENTS

I would like to acknowledge the individuals and organizations that have given so generously to this work. The Friends of the Windham Historic Commission have supported this project and provided several of the images. Proceeds from this work will go toward the restoration of the Searles School and Chapel. Dennis Root has for many years sought out and preserved old images of Windham and has generously provided many of the photographs and postcard views presented here. Pam Skinner and Tracy Johnson both made their collections of postcards available. Peter Griffin was instrumental in acquiring many images and offered the use of his personal collection of photographs and postcards. The collection of photographs by Baldwin Coolidge held by the Society for the Preservation of New England Antiquities (SPNEA) has contributed a very real sense of what Windham was like in the early 1880s. Lorna Condon and Sally Hinkle, archivists at the SPNEA, were generous with their time and resources. Eugene Gaddis, archivist of the Wadsworth Atheneum and curator of the Austin house, in Hartford, Connecticut, made available the Atheneum's collection of Windham Playhouse photographs.

Those who contributed photographs and shared their personal recollections include Marija Sanderling and John Barrett (at the Nesmith Library), Bob and Shirley Armstrong, Alan Armstrong, Gary Armstrong, Tom Furlong, Joe Bella, Mary Glance, Cindy Amato, Charlene Kane, Paul and Ruth Smith, Herb Crucius, Richard and Connie McKinley, Fred Linnemann, Phyllis Churchill, Carol Webber, Bud Travis, Tom and Anne Wilson, Mary Massa, Jimmy Brown, Dianne Gulden, Lyn O'Loughlin, Nancy Drummond, Phil and Beverly Meuse, Ted Dooley, Bill and Cathy Wallace, Dorothy West, Janice Rioux, John and Sandra Mangan, Patricia Dingivan, Jean Normington, Shirley Pivovar, Kevin Waterhouse, Mabel Corson, Joe and Sue Alosky, Gail Souza, Paul and Judy Strathie, Barbara Fellows, Shirley Beaulieu, Bob Skinner, Wendy Devlin, and Elaine Keefe. Willis Low and Charlie Butterfield provided personal insights about the town's past. Bob Thorndike presented surveys of historic resources. Maria Webber, my first-grade teacher at the Searles School, provided information about Windham's past and is a role model for living life well. George and Marion Dinsmore have supported this project and have worked tirelessly over the years in efforts to preserve Windham's history. The most difficult task of this entire project was selecting which of all the wonderful images would appear.

If you enjoy the photographs and history presented here, please remember to support the preservation efforts of the Windham Historic Commission, the Windham Historical Society, the Windham Museum, and the Society for the Preservation of New England Antiquities. Once historic photographs, buildings, and artifacts are gone, they can never be replaced.

INTRODUCTION

The Scotch-Irish settlers who arrived in 1719 were so taken by this place that they built their homes here, defying the representatives of the British Crown who had hoped to plant them in the wilds of Maine as a bulwark against the American Indians. They called the place Nutfield because of the abundance of nut-bearing trees. A vibrant community grew up based on Presbyterian orthodoxy, fine linens, and country fairs. The poet John Greenleaf Whittier described the new community this way:

> In a few years they had cleared large fields, built substantial stone and frame dwellings, and a large commodious meetinghouse; wealth had accumulated around them, and they everywhere had the reputation of a shrewd and thriving community. Their moral acclimation in Ireland had not been without its effect upon their character. Side by side with Presbyterianism as austere as that of John Knox had grown something of the wild Milesian humor, love of convivial excitement and merrymaking. Their long prayers and fierce zeal in behalf of the orthodox tenants only served, in the eyes of their Puritan neighbors, to make more glaring still the scandal of their marked social irregularities. It was said in the region round about that the Derry Presbyterians would never give up a pint of doctrine or a pint of rum.

In regard to the fairs held there, Whittier said that they were characterized by "a wild, frolicking, drinking, fiddling, courting, horse-racing, riotous merrymaking; a sort of protestant carnival, relaxing the grimness of Puritanism for leagues around." Every farmer grew a field of flax that was then threshed and broken. The mothers and daughters would spin and then weave fine linen by the firelight, into sheets and tablecloths that were coveted for their uncompromising quality.

In 1728, the Windham Range was laid out on a swell of land that ran between Cobbett's Pond and Canobie Lake. Soon, farms appeared with well-tended fields and pastures running to the shoreline. In 1742, the time came for Windham to go its own way and to sever itself from Londonderry. A meetinghouse was soon built on a hill in the Range overlooking Cobbett's Pond. Simon Williams nurtured his flock here, and life centered on farming, church, and family. The experience of owning their own land and enjoying the fruit of their labor was an intoxicating brew of self-empowerment. These Scotch immigrants had suffered the great injustice of being tenant farmers in Northern Ireland. Many had lost everything or seen their lives laid low by the racketeering landlords who had raised their rents after they had made all the improvements to the land. The London merchants who owned the land in Northern Ireland owed their fortunes to the power of the king. When talk of revolution hit the colonies, the people of Windham were more than ready to fight for their newfound freedom and lash out at the corrupt system that had robbed them in the past.

As the town grew and prospered, there was a call for the meetinghouse to be moved to a more central location. Surveyor John Caldwell determined the exact center of town and drove a stake in the ground. Here, in 1798, a new meetinghouse was built. Soon this became the social, civic, religious, and economic center of the town. The population grew until it reached the milestone of 1,000. Then one of those great turning points of history hit.

The industrial city of Lowell was built on the Merrimack River, and the sons and daughters of Windham farmers began migrating to the city for its well-paying jobs. Everything in Lowell was new and exciting. Here and in other growing cities, one could make a fortune, and several Windham natives did. Many others were caught in the tide flowing to the vast fertile lands of the West. Windham's population declined steadily, and many farms were simply abandoned. Time seemed to stand still as generations passed, surrounded by the quiet rhythms of country life.

In the 1840s, the first railroad passed through Windham. Soon another line ran through town that met at the Junction. Stations were built at West Windham and Canobie Lake, and villages sprang up around them. City folk from the nearby industrial centers soon discovered how easy it was to escape the crowded conditions and spend a day or week in these beautiful surroundings. New businesses grew up to cater to these tourists. Dozens of boardinghouses operated, and picnic groves were established on the lakes for day-trippers. Farmers prospered, as they were able to ship what they produced to the nearby cities, and the sawmills hummed with activity as the abundant cash crop of newly fallen trees filled hundreds of railroad cars leaving town.

Everyone has fantasized about being able to travel back in time in order to experience an important historical event or to simply see a place as it was in the past. We imagine what a place was like and conjure up the faces of people and wonder how they lived their lives. We long to hear their voices and know their stories. The images captured through the lens of a camera have the ability to draw us back in time. In an instant, a scene, a face, or a great event is held tightly in place, frozen for future generations to marvel at and enjoy. In this book, you will discover Windham, New Hampshire, as you never imagined. It was a place of quiet country roads, beautiful farms, unspoiled lakes and ponds, and the ever-present backdrop of striking scenery. The photographic odyssey begins in the 1880s, when Baldwin Coolidge traveled from Boston to Windham by train, with a large cumbersome camera that required a heavy tripod for support and that used fragile glass plates to record the photographs. His artistic eye captured haunting images of the way life had been for much of the 19th century.

Other compelling photographs bring the forgotten villages at the Junction, West Windham and Canobie Lake back to life. Be captivated by the farms, mills, boardinghouses, stores, and lakeside picnic groves. Look into the faces of the people who made up this tight-knit community. Watch as cottages and businesses are built along the shores of Cobbett's Pond and Canobie Lake, and have a glimpse at the rites and rituals of summer.

See why multimillionaire Edward Francis Searles was so taken with the panoramic views and natural beauty on the ridges of Jenny's Hill and Dinsmoor's Hill that he purchased more than 1,300 acres of land there. Tour the medieval castle that his flights of fancy brought forth and that forever changed the face of Windham. Finally, be dazzled by the Windham Playhouse as told through stunning photographs of cast and crew and the magnificent stage sets that were the hallmark of this popular summer theater. See how Chick Austin, with the glamour and style that surrounded him, filled this unassuming town with a radiant presence.

So sit down, relax, turn off your cell phone, and get carried back in time. Leave the place you know behind, the place Interstate 93 transformed from a small country town into an affluent Boston suburb. Return to a community where everyone knows your name and where farms and open space are commonplace. Clear your mind of traffic jams and the breakneck pace of modern life. Yes, it is time to return to a simpler way of life and to discover Windham as it once was.

One

A TIMELESS INTERLUDE

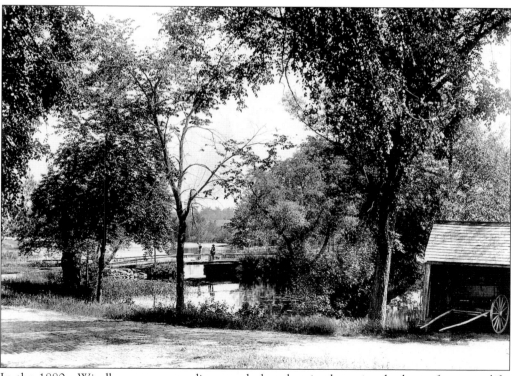

In the 1880s, Windham was an undiscovered place lost in the quiet rhythms of country life. The town's unspoiled setting was the inspiration for the noted photographer Baldwin Coolidge. His photographic artistry captures Windham as a vision of pastoral beauty. These compelling images will draw you back in time. (Baldwin Coolidge No. 161-B; courtesy of SPNEA.)

Baldwin Coolidge was a leading Boston photographer who created thousands of memorable images. He was a staff photographer at the Museum of Fine Arts for more than 30 years and billed himself as "an artist." His beautiful photographs surely bestow this title upon him. He captured the essence of the New England landscape both in Boston and in many rural and seacoast communities in Massachusetts, New Hampshire, and southern Maine. The stories behind these images provide a valuable lesson about the need to support the work of historic preservation. All of these very early views of Windham might have been lost if it had not been for the foresight of William Sumner Appleton in acquiring the glass-plate negatives of Baldwin Coolidge in 1918. Appleton founded the Society for the Preservation of New England Antiquities (SPNEA) to preserve New England's past for the benefit of future generations. This portrait is by John H. Garo. (Courtesy of SPNEA.)

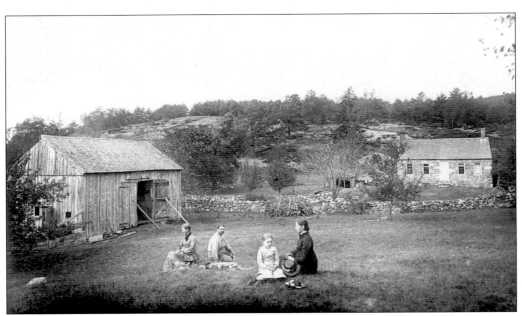

The Clendenin farm was located on the Windham-Derry line. This handsome fieldstone house was built in 1736. Many of these early stone houses were used as garrisons during the Indian wars. Take note of the high stone walls. The house still stands on Goodhue Road. The people posing for Coolidge are unidentified. (Baldwin Coolidge No. 3004; courtesy of SPNEA.)

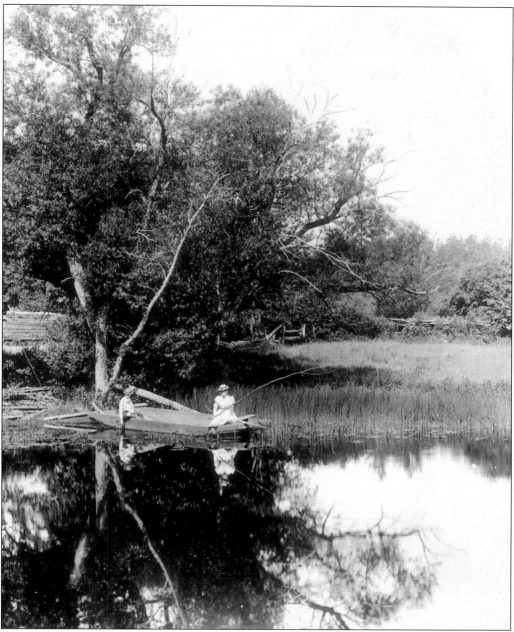

A young woman and a boy fishing from a boat on Kendall's Mill Pond present an idyllic summer scene. The beautiful image captures the reflection of the willows on the water. Kendall's Mill Pond was a popular spot with summer boarders who could rent a boat and fish or collect the fragrant water lilies that grew there. (Baldwin Coolidge No. 160-B; courtesy of SPNEA.)

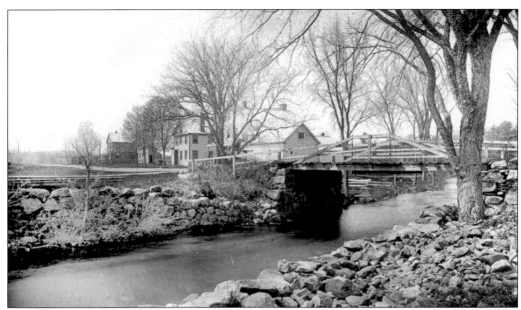

The village of West Windham first developed because of the waterpower supplied by Beaver Brook and the construction of a major highway. Henry Campbell erected the first mill in 1750. Mammoth Road was built in 1831 and ran from Lowell, Massachusetts, to Hooksett, New Hampshire. The turnpike ran across this bridge in West Windham not far from the three-story factory that A.R. Burnham built in 1836. Bartley, Underhill & Company opened a store in the 1830s, and the first post office opened in 1844. Construction began on the Nashua & Rochester Railroad in 1872, and trains began running in 1874. The station built in West Windham spurred more growth by creating a convenient place for summer boarders to reach from the nearby cities. (Baldwin Coolidge No. 272-A [above] and No. 263-A [below]; courtesy of SPNEA.)

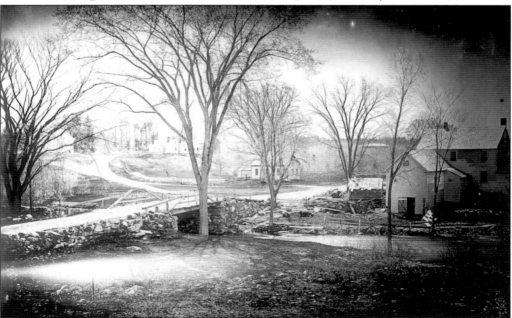

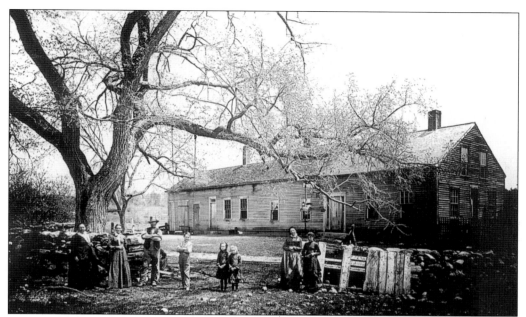

The Clark farm was located on Kendall Pond Road. The large elm tree was known as "the horse whip tree." Samuel Clark pulled a sapling from the ground to use as a whip. According to legend, he later replanted it in his yard, and it grew into this magnificent tree. The sparks from a passing train set the surrounding fields and house ablaze in 1912. Pictured here are, from left to right, Evelyn, Joanna, Henry, George, Angeline, unidentified, Joanna, and Rosa. (Baldwin Coolidge No. 155-B; courtesy of SPNEA.)

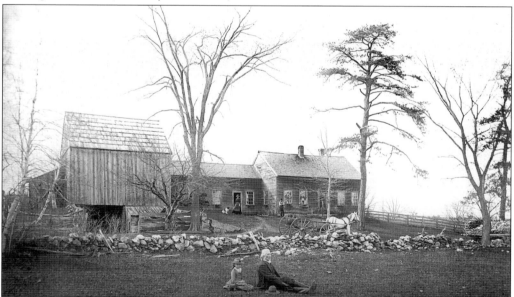

Jacob Barker, a wheelwright, carpenter, and farmer, built this home in 1828. In this photograph from the 1880s, Jacob sits in the field with a girl who is likely a granddaughter. His son Charles, with his wife, Amelia, stands near the house; their horse and wagon are parked on Mammoth Road. (Baldwin Coolidge No. 271-A; courtesy of SPNEA.)

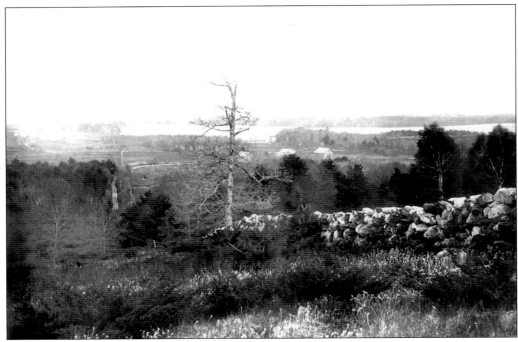

This view looks toward the southeast from Dinsmoor's Hill. Canobie Lake is in the distance along with the Leonard Morrison farm and the brick Schoolhouse No. 1. Pastures and stone walls climb the slopes. The multimillionaire Edward Searles later built his castle near this spot. (Baldwin Coolidge No. 162-B; courtesy of SPNEA.)

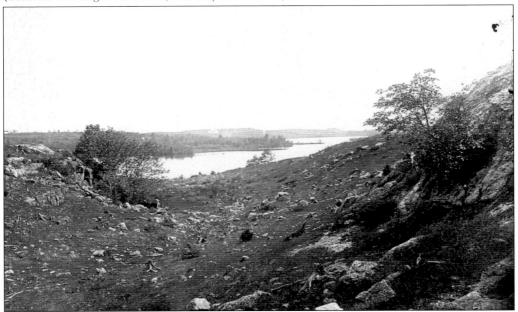

The Rocky Pasture offered a panoramic view of Cobbett's Pond. In the early 1880s, there was not a single summer cottage to be found on this pristine lake. Frank Ayer built the first cottage here in 1886. (Baldwin Coolidge No. 279-A; courtesy of SPNEA.)

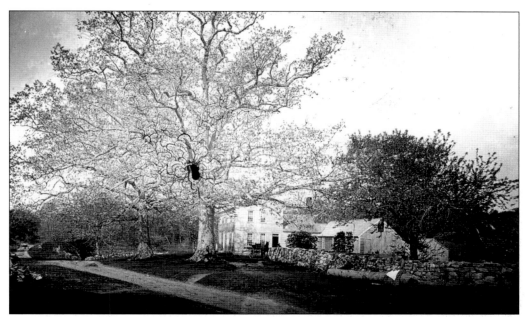

The Park homestead was built in 1742. Elder Robert Park left two oaks for shade in his front yard after clearing his land, and they grew to a massive size with great, spreading branches. Mary Ellen Parks sits on a log, and her brother John stands near the horse and wagon. The house is still on Range Road. (Baldwin Coolidge No. 254-A; courtesy of SPNEA.)

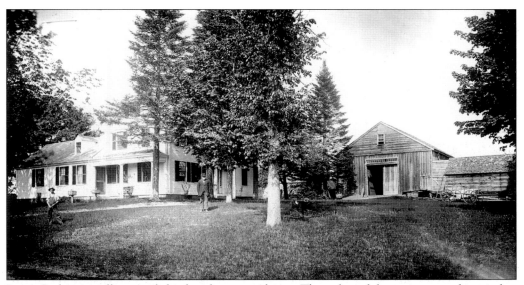

James Park originally owned this handsome residence. The value of the property and its timber increased substantially when the city of Lowell was built. Park moved to Lowell in 1868 and sold the farm to Isaac P. Cochran. In this photograph, Cochran stands near the tree, and his son John is closer to the road. Isaac's wife, Martha, sits under the tree with an unidentified woman. The house burned at the beginning of the 20th century, but the barn and a later Cochran house still stand on North Lowell Road. (Baldwin Coolidge No. 266-A; courtesy of SPNEA.)

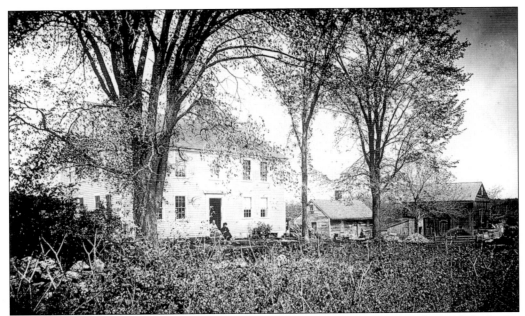

Joseph Armstrong, a hatter by trade, purchased this property from James Clyde in 1827. At the time this photograph was taken in the 1880s, his grandson Joseph C. Armstrong occupied the farm with his sister Sarah Ann. Known later as Echo Farm, it was located just past the school near the center. (Baldwin Coolidge No. 306-A; courtesy of SPNEA.)

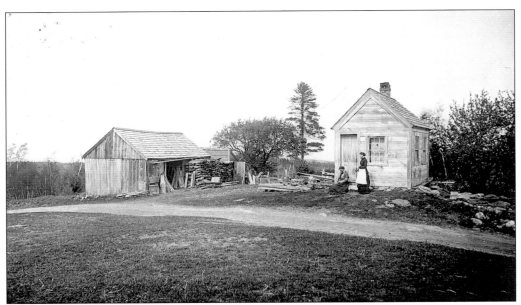

Nothing is recorded in Windham's history about Miss Newell or the location of her farm. This charming photograph invokes all sorts of beguiling questions about her and the life she led on the crest of this hill in Windham. Who was she? Who was the other woman? How did she survive on this tiny farm? All the questions go unanswered, but the image remains. (Baldwin Coolidge No. 274-A; courtesy of SPNEA.)

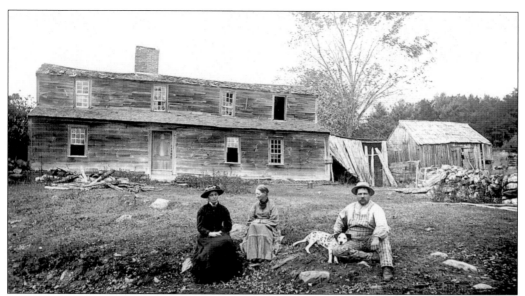

The cellar holes and stone walls found in the woods throughout Windham are the remnants of once-thriving farms. A great exodus began in the 1820s to the vast fertile lands of the West and to the nearby industrial cities. The population in Windham peaked in 1830 at 1,006 people and declined steadily until 1890, when just over 600 people lived here. Many men from Windham were employed in the construction of the dam and canal in Lowell, Massachusetts. The money to be made in the city enticed them to leave town. The mill hands who occupied the neat boardinghouses were the refined and well-educated daughters of New England farmers. Morrison states, "Everything was changed; friends, neighbors, kindred were gone; the houses fallen into decay, and the farms deserted. Today, in 1882, the old cellars and door-stones alone remain, in the dense woods, or fields, or pastures, to mark the place where once were hospitable homes and well cultivated farms." The above photograph depicts the ruins of the Shields place. The photograph below shows the Haskell farm. Both the people and the locations of these abandoned farms are unidentified. (Baldwin Coolidge No. 244-A [above] and No. 259-A [below]; courtesy of SPNEA.)

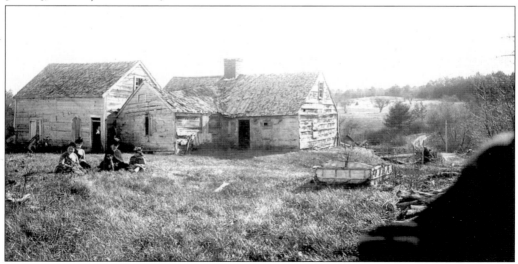

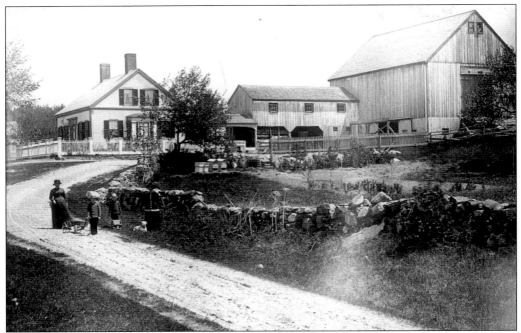

This beautiful farm, built in 1815 by Samuel W. Simpson, was located on Range Road in south Windham. Samuel's grandniece Eva (Simpson) Cutting is shown here in the 1880s with her two boys, Charles and John. The second woman is unidentified. Beehives can be seen in the center. (Baldwin Coolidge No. 156-B; courtesy of SPNEA.)

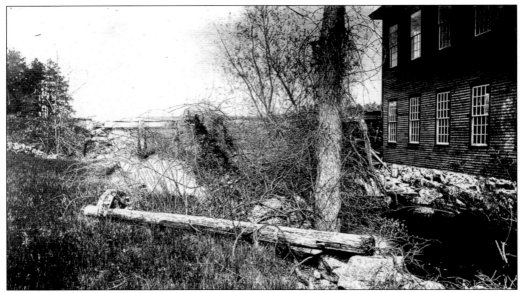

The old mill in south Windham was the only large manufacturing building built in town during the 19th century. It was powered with water from Cobbett's Pond. A wooden gear lies abandoned near the dam. (Baldwin Coolidge No. 270-A; courtesy of SPNEA.)

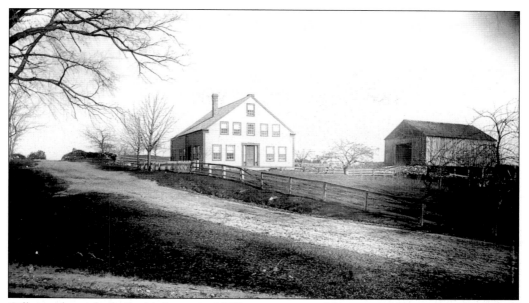

Gilbert Alexander built this house in 1835 on a portion of the original Nesmith farm. His son Charles owned the farm when this photograph was taken. The house still stands on North Lowell Road and was for many years the residence of the Low family. (Baldwin Coolidge No. 258-A; courtesy of SPNEA.)

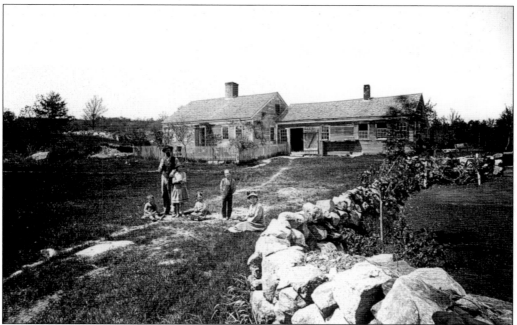

James Betton was a farmer, surveyor, and auctioneer who built this home in 1753. He presided over 20 town meetings and was both a delegate at the Provincial Congress at Exeter and an agent to the Continental Congress in Philadelphia. Pictured is a later owner of the farm, Albert Campbell, with his wife, Josephine, and their children, John, Mabel, Viola, and Charles. The home still exists on Londonderry Road. (Baldwin Coolidge No. 154-B; courtesy of SPNEA.)

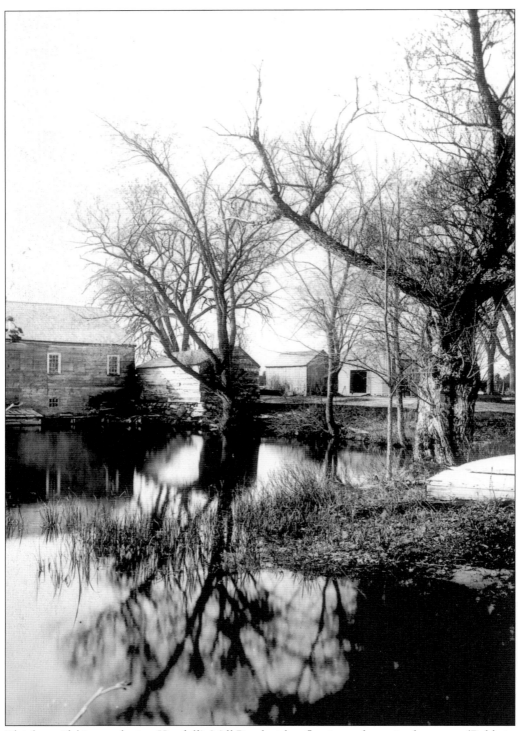

This beautiful image depicts Kendall's Mill Pond with reflections of trees in the water. (Baldwin Coolidge No. 246-A; courtesy of SPNEA.)

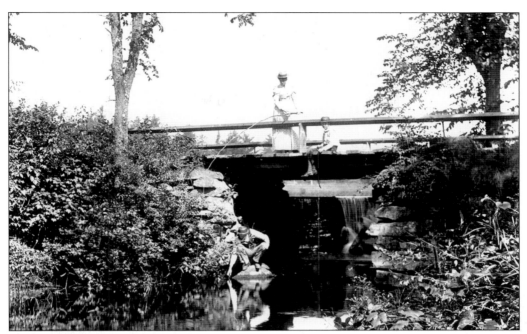

The Kendall's Mill Pond Bridge, located on the Windham-Londonderry line, was built in 1760. The dam can be seen behind the bridge. (Baldwin Coolidge No. 157-B; courtesy of SPNEA.)

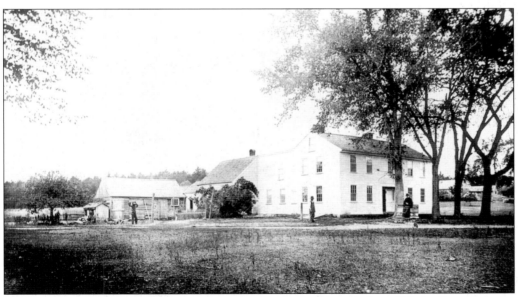

Capt. William Moore, who fought at Bunker Hill, was the first member of his family to own the land and mill. In 1742, when the town was divided, the family's house was in Windham, and much of their land and mill was in Londonderry. This home was built later and was known as the Old Kendall House. The man and woman standing in front are likely Everett and Harriet Kendall. Notice the unusual double-door front entry. (Baldwin Coolidge No. 248-A; courtesy of SPNEA.)

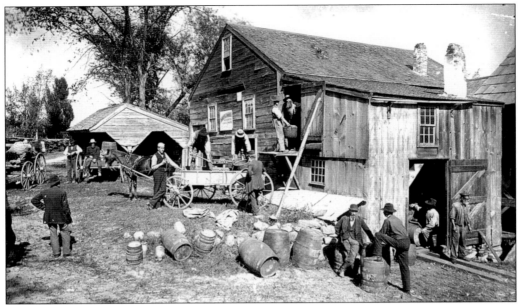

In 1751, water privileges were granted to Benjamin Wilson, who built the first mill here. The mill was later known variously as Moor's, Goss, and Kendall's. Everett Kendall operated a grist, cider, and sawmill here for many years. Apples were an important cash crop for farmers, who brought them to mills like this to be pressed into cider. Kendall had a large storage building near the mill where he aged the cider. Cider making was a social event for the local farmers, as evidenced by the large group gathered around the mill. As apples are removed from a wagon in baskets, cider is sampled by many of the people gathered around the mill. (Baldwin Coolidge No. 473-A [above] and No. 283-A [below]; courtesy of SPNEA.)

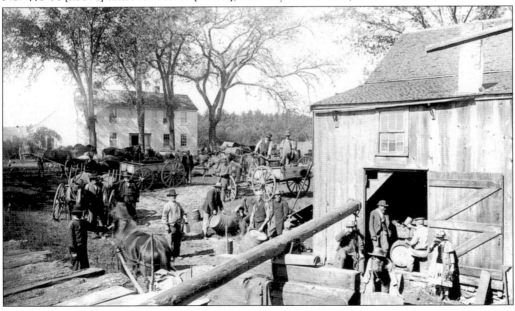

Two
WINDHAM CENTER

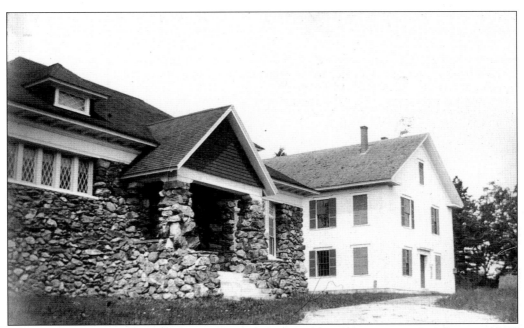

Windham Center was established 56 years after the founding of the town in 1742. Prior to 1798, the meetinghouse had been located in the Range. It stood in the Cemetery on the Hill, with the early settlers buried around it. The Range had been laid out in 1728 and was the first area to be settled. As people began to establish farms in other parts of town, pressure mounted to move the meetinghouse to a more central location. In 1792, John Caldwell completed a survey and then drove a stake at the exact center of town. The meetinghouse was constructed in 1798, making the structure the religious, governmental, social, and commercial center of town.

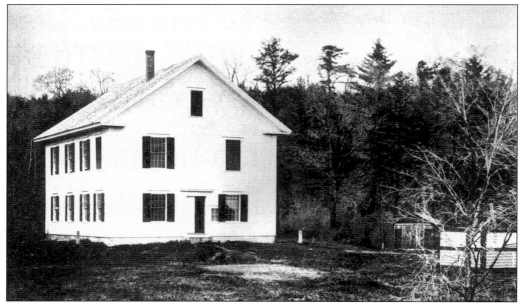

The meetinghouse at the center was raised on July 5, 1798. The selectmen invited 80 men to raise the building and furnished them with victuals and drink, which included plenty of New England rum. The building opened to the second floor, with the Palladian window behind the pulpit. Porches were at each gable end. In 1865, the town house was turned a quarter round to its present position. In 1868, the building was extensively remodeled, and the interior was divided into upper and lower halls, a library, and a selectmen's room.

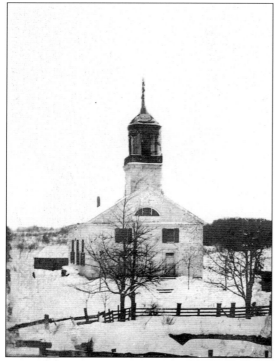

The earliest photographic image known to exist of the town of Windham is this copy of a daguerreotype owned by Mrs. Albert Farmer, taken *c.* 1862. The two small trees were set out in front of the church in 1861. The Windham Presbyterian Church was built in 1834, a beautiful example of the Federal style, with small-paned windows and the absence of a window between the doors. At the time of this photograph, there was a railing (no longer in existence) around the top of the steeple.

Windham has always taken the time to celebrate its past. The town honors two important events: the anniversary celebration for the founding of the town in 1742 and the anniversary celebration for the founding of Ancient Nutfield by the early Scotch-Irish settlers in 1719. To the right, a poster announces the 200th-anniversary celebration of Nutfield in 1919. Nutfield covered a huge area and consisted of the towns of Windham, Derry, Londonderry, and parts of Manchester, Hudson, and Salem. Pictured below are some of the 400 people who were served a chicken dinner at the 200th anniversary in 1942. In spite of the fact that World War II was raging in Europe and the Pacific, the people of Windham found time to celebrate the founding of the town. In 1942, just 735 people lived in Windham. Mark your calendars for the next Nutfield celebration, in 2019, and the next Windham anniversary celebration, in 2042.

1719-1919

ANCIENT NUTFIELD

Comprising **DERRY, LONDONDERRY, WINDHAM,** and parts of **MANCHESTER, HUDSON** and **SALEM**

WILL CELEBRATE THE

TWO HUNDREDTH ANNIVERSARY

OF ITS SETTLEMENT

SUNDAY - MONDAY - TUESDAY
Aug. 24   Aug. 25   Aug. 26

. . . **PROGRAM** . . .

SUNDAY···Union Service at East Derry in the afternoon.
MONDAY···8 and 6: Parade of Horribles, Ball Game, Grand Parade, Aeroplane Exhibition, Carnival of Sports at West Derry.
    EVENING: Historical Pageant at Derry Village.
TUESDAY···10.00 and 1.30: Historical Address, Oration, Speaking by Invited Guests at West Derry.
    EVENING: Fireworks.

MUSIC AT ALL TIMES | MAKE YOUR PLANS TO COME

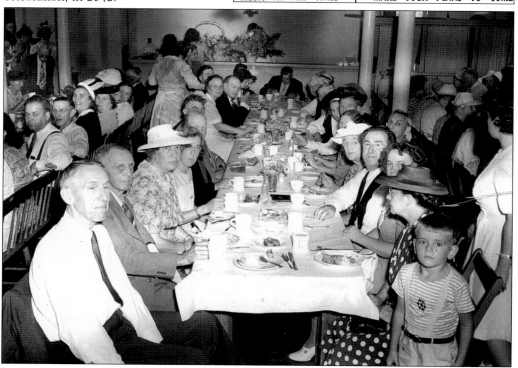

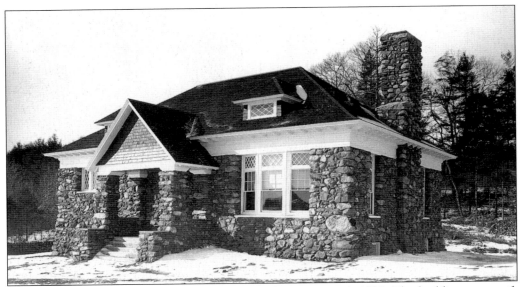

The Armstrong Memorial Building was dedicated on January 4, 1899. The building was a gift from George Washington Armstrong to house the Nesmith Library. Col. Thomas Nesmith, a successful businessman in Lowell and a Windham native, gave $3,000 for the establishment of a free public library. Nesmith Library opened on June 21, 1871, in a room set aside for the purpose in the town hall. This beautiful fieldstone building was designed by William W. Dinsmoor of Boston. These photographs were taken at the opening of the building. In the photograph below, the donor's portrait hangs on the wall, and oil lamps used for illumination are pictured.

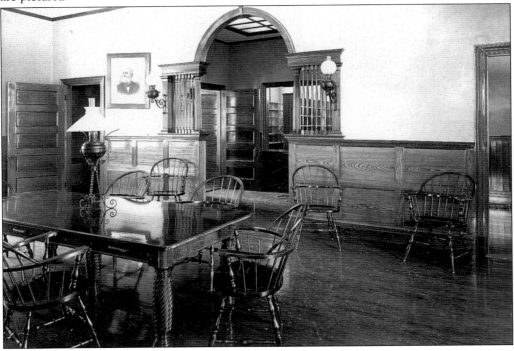

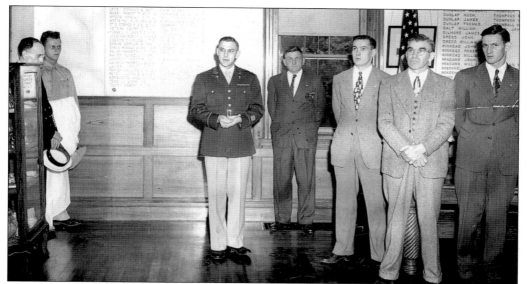

The marble plaque at Nesmith Library honors the 79 Windham men (nearly 10 percent of the population) who served in World War II. Bob Armstrong is pictured second from the left in the corner with other veterans at the dedication ceremony. Maurice Tarbell is standing second from the right. His son Wilbur was the only casualty of the war from Windham. He was killed while serving aboard the USS *Scorpion*, which sank while on patrol in the Yellow Sea in 1944.

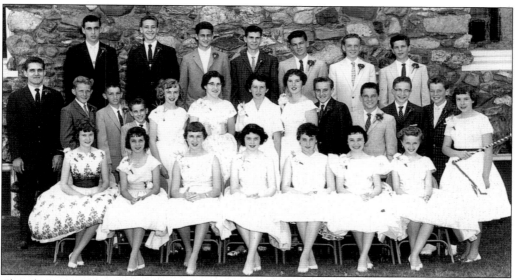

The class of 1959 poses in front of the library on graduation from eighth grade. From left to right are the following: (front row) Nancy Barlow, Roberta Downing, Kathleen Short, Patricia Matte, Gail Travis, Sharon Tammany, Ruth Scott, and Linda Loranger (with baton); (middle row) Jack Bone, Richard Bone, Gary Armstrong, Richard Horton, Nancy Low, Carol Corbin, Nan Holm, Joanna Boda, William Brown, James Perry, Clifford Chadwick, and Paul Foden; (back row) Richard Wescott, Dennis Root, William Crucius, Robert Clay, Roger Binette, and Vincent Waterhouse.

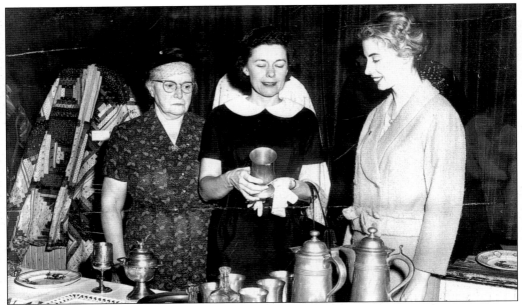

The Windites, an offshoot of the Windham Woman's Club, were young mothers meeting in the evening. Freida Sheldon (left), first lady Beverly Powell (center), and Marion Dinsmore examine artifacts of Old Fort No. 4 during a coffee hour at the town hall in 1960.

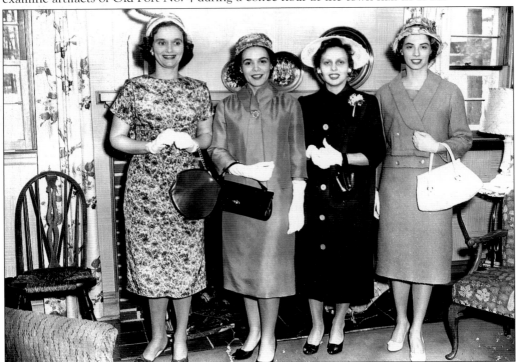

Posing with fashions that won a statewide sewing contest in 1959 are, from left to right, Marion Winmill, Simone Mason, Shirley Armstrong, and Marion Dinsmore. The Windites were an active women's club from 1948 through the 1960s.

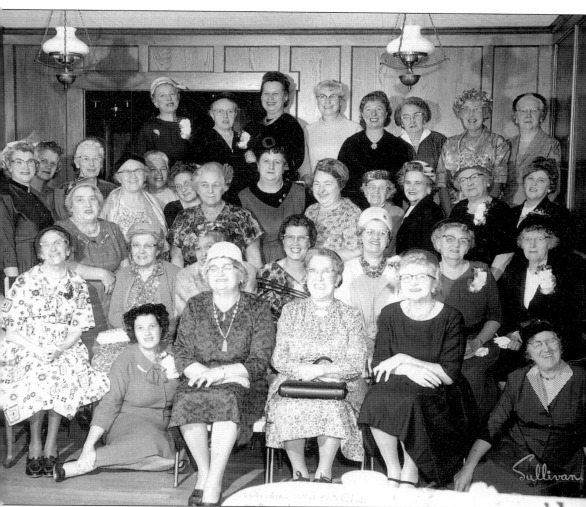

This photograph was taken in 1961 on the 50th anniversary of the Windham Woman's Club. The club was organized in 1911 through the efforts of a group of women headed by Julia Baker. It became a member of the Federation of New Hampshire Woman's Clubs in 1912. In the beginning, club activities centered on social events like automobile outings, bundle parties, May nights, and strawberry festivals. Later, the group became more involved in community affairs and is still active today. Members pictured here are, from left to right, as follows: (first row) Rose Boda, Ethel Robinson, Janet Haigh, Mae Miers, and Helen Lamson; (second row) Helen Rogers, Fanny Perry, Louise Rupf, Justine Andrews, Dorothy Westcott, Ruth Lovell, Marion Evans, and Elva Tarbell; (third row) Minnie Moore, Florence Cross, Peal Gage, Cora Bourque, Ann Bailey, Bertha Kannheiser, Emma Demarais, Emma Hardy, Dorothy Gordon, Rose Mason, Marion Boden, Lillian Leeman, and Hellen Furneaux; (fourth row) Ruth Crocker, Freida Sheldon, Mary Wallace, Dorothy Butterfield, Laura Marquebruck, Ida Myers, Caroline Cochran, and Mabel Peabody.

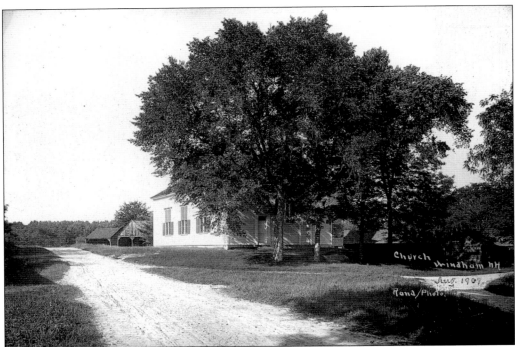

In the early days, Windham was a Presbyterian theocracy. With the passage of the Toleration Act on July 1, 1819, the practice of taxing local citizens for the support of the church came to an end. The Presbyterian Religious Society raised $2,450 through subscriptions and the sale of pews. In 1834, the new church was raised from June 27 through June 29. Much was made of the fact that the structure was built without the requisite aid of alcoholic spirits. The Reverend Loren Thayer led the dedication ceremony on January 14, 1835. In 1874, the building was extensively remodeled to reflect the tastes of the Victorian era. The above photograph, taken in 1907, shows the old carriage sheds. Below, Lowell Road is pictured in a view looking south.

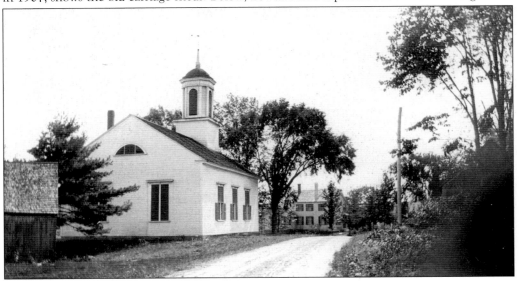

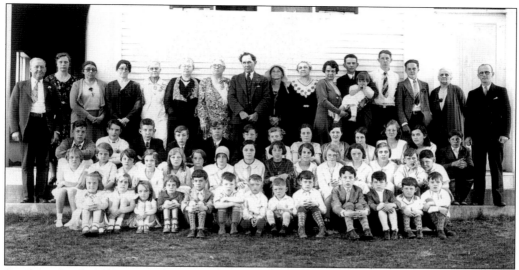

Sunday school children and their teachers pose in 1932 in front of the church. Some of the people identified but not listed in order include the following: (first row) Dorothy Gould, Rusell Lamson, Wesley Lamson, Fred Low, Charlie Gould, and Bobby Low; (second row) Mary Waterhouse, Charlotte Harris, Grace Eason, Harriet Gould, Barbara Lamson, Dot Teriella, and Jack Lamson; (third row) Bill Moeckel, Bob Mason, Chester Johnson, John Tariella, and Harriet Low; (fourth row) Tellis Wells, Florence Garland, Francis Dow, Thomas and Mrs. Waterhouse, Ken Holms's sister, Ken Holms, and Rev. M.B. Crist.

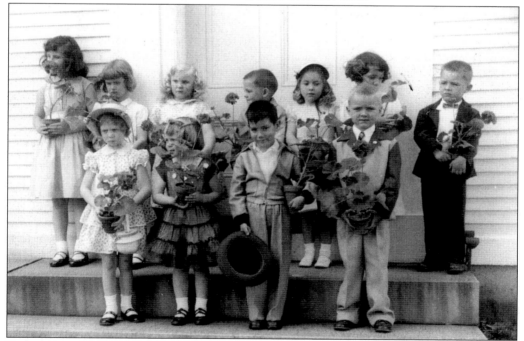

Pictured on Children's Day in 1954 are, from left to right, the following: (front row) Sally Shumaker, Ruth Herbert, Jack McClennan, and Paul Root; (back row) Linda Glance, Mary Lou Holms, Barbara Moeckel, Donald Travis, Cheryl Hamer, Mary Devlin, and Alan Armstrong.

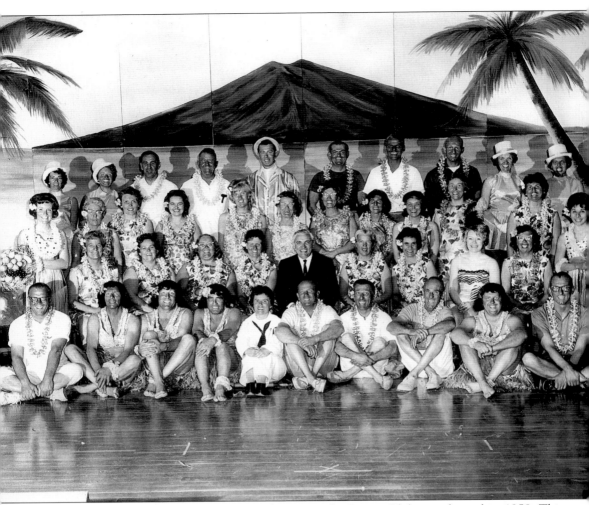

The Presbyterian Couples Club, better known as the Presco Club, was formed in 1958. This very active group often held fundraisers for the Presbyterian church. When putting on a show, all of the members pitched in and had an active role. The photograph above is from the show *Island Holiday*. The South Pacific–themed show was a great success. The beautiful scenery was designed and painted by Diane Gulden. The players were all local people who put on costumes and hit the stage singing and dancing. The cast and crew of *Island Holiday* are, from left to right, as follows: (first row) unidentified, George Armstrong, Elly Sypher, Sox Brunt, Bea Polak, Ed Herbert, Jerry Dearborn, Leo Root, John McKinnon, and Rev. John Mahler; (second row) unidentified, Dottie (Moulton) Radcliffe, Barbara Root, Dottie (Lamson) Zanca, Peter Spampanato, Jane Dearborn, Barbara Sypher, unidentified, Barbara McKinnon, and unidentified; (third row) unidentified, Nan Milligan, five unidentified people, Shirley Beaulieu, Diane Gulden, Nancy Roberts, and Margie Brunt; (fourth row) Dot Armstrong, Barbara Coish, Cliff Marshall, John Milligan, Rudy Pivovar, Bill Gulden, Bob Armstrong, Billy Roberts, Maryann Drake, and Shirley Armstrong.

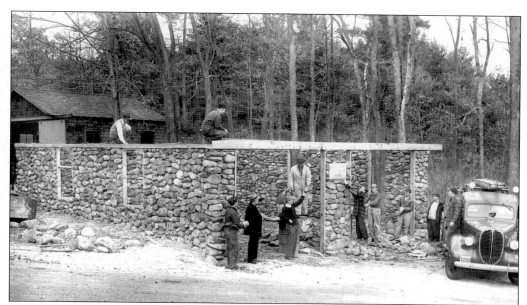

Construction of the first firehouse took place in November 1946. Volunteer firemen, who often worked at night, built it with the aid of floodlights. The old fire barn is shown behind the new building. Chief James Brown places the granite plaque. Shown in the photograph are, from left to right, Albert Rioux and George Gagnon (on the wall), Fred Low, Willis Low, George Webster, Eugene Zins, Chief Brown, Edward Herbert, Fred Bestany, 2nd Lt. Jess Perry, and Robert Low (on the fire truck). District fire chief Merton Webber also volunteered his services.

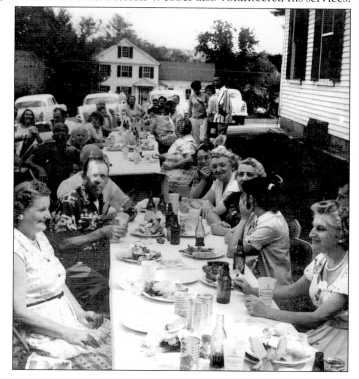

The fire department held many fundraising events at the center, including the annual carnival with fortune tellers and games of chance. Enjoying a fire department picnic beside the town hall in the 1950s are, from left to right, Jim Zins, Iola Zins, Eleanor Zins, Maggie Zins, Muriel Bistany, Harriet Low, and Betty Moeckel.

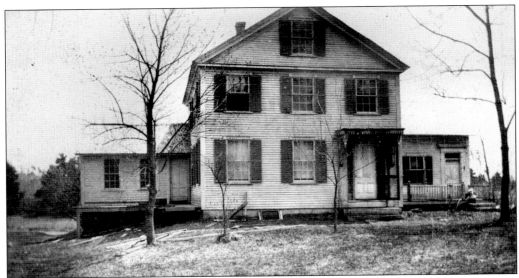

The Robert Bartley house was built in the Greek Revival style *c.* 1856. Bartley was a local merchant who moved to Windham in 1833. He bought the house and the business from the Nesmith brothers, who had operated a store here since 1815. Both the original house and the store burned in 1856. In addition to his store in the center, Bartley also operated a store in West Windham. In later years, Anne Clark operated a boardinghouse here known as Nine Acres.

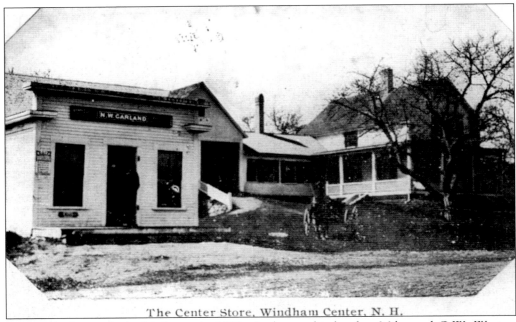

The Center Store, Windham Center, N. H.

Horace Anderson built this house in 1861. Anderson, his brother Milo, and G.W. Weston operated Weston & Anderson, a shoemaking company. Anderson's second wife, Isadore Burnham, was one of the first five women to vote at a school district meeting in 1889. Later, Nathaniel Garland operated a store from this location (shown above).

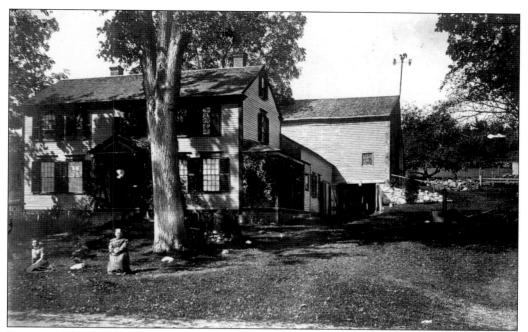

Benjamin Blanchard, a carpenter, built this home in 1820. Dr. Ira Weston purchased the house in 1848 and practiced medicine here. John Dalton and Sophia Warren owned the house from 1874 to 1901 and are shown sitting on the lawn above.

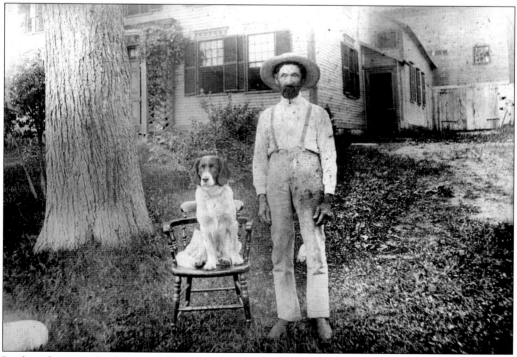

In this photograph, the seat of honor belongs to John Dalton Warren's beloved dog.

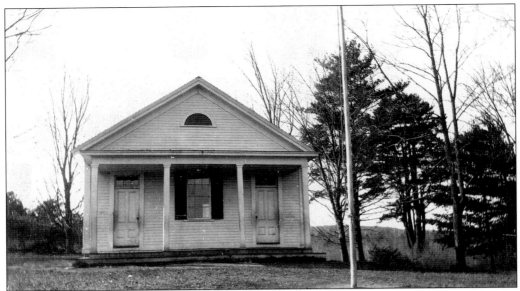

The No. 6 Schoolhouse was located near the present location of Center School. It was built in 1857 at a cost of $1,200 and replaced an earlier schoolhouse at the same location. It was moved across Lowell Road when Center School was built in 1939 and is now a comfortable home. Thayer Pine can be seen in the background. The giant tree had its top blown off in the great gale of 1815 and was saved from the ax by the Reverend Loren Thayer.

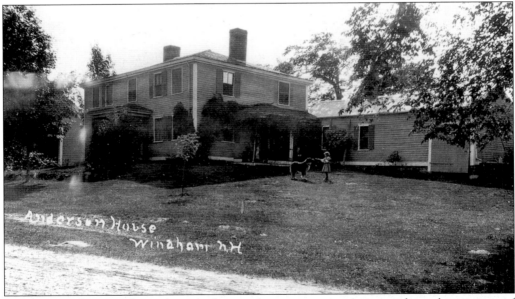

The Reverend Loren Thayer house is known for its most prominent resident, the minister of the Presbyterian church from 1845 to 1866. The Federal-style Colonial was built c. 1811 by Jacob Johnson. David Anderson owned the property at the time of this photograph and started a poultry farm that remained in his family until 1935.

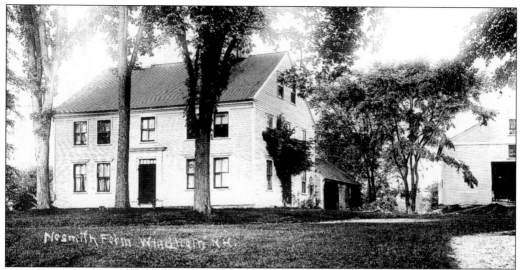

Robert Park may have built this house as early as the 1750s. Col. Jacob Nesmith purchased the farm in 1820. A commander in the 8th Regiment of New Hampshire Militia, he married Margaret Dinsmoor and had eight children. The home remained in the Nesmith family until 1945.

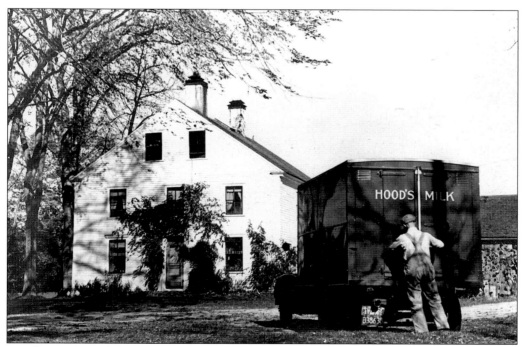

Hood's was one of the dairies that purchased milk produced in Windham. In the early days, milk was shipped by rail to the H.P. Hood Creamery in South Lawrence, Massachusetts. In this photograph from the 1930s, milk is picked up by truck at the Nesmith farm.

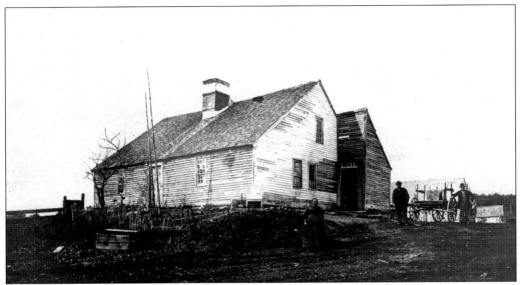

This center-chimney Cape was built c. 1762 by Deacon John Armstrong. It replaced an earlier house that had been built by John Archibald. Armstrong was a weaver from Londonderry, Ireland, and had immigrated to America with his father. His son David followed him on the farm and married Elizabeth Hemphill. They had 12 children together. The farm remained in the Armstrong family until the early 20th century. It is still standing on Londonderry Road.

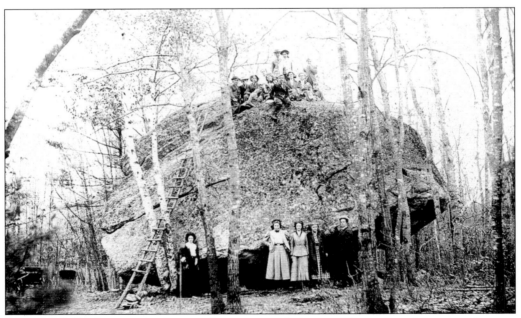

Butterfield's Rock was a popular spot for outings and pictures. The rock took its name from an old hunter named Butterfield, who, in the early 1700s, used to camp beneath its overhanging sides. Because the rock was situated high on a hill, a climb up the ladder was rewarded with panoramic views.

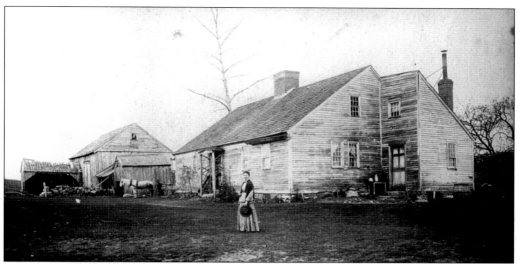

Robert Hemphill built the Hemphill-Merrill house as early as 1765. He was one of 99 Windham men who signed the Association Test in April 1776. By signing, the men promised to risk their lives and fortunes in defense of the United American Colonies against the British army. Mary Ellenwood Hemphill married Giles Merrill, and they then became the owners of this farm. Their daughter Lydia stands in front of this handsome center-chimney Cape that was once on North Lowell Road.

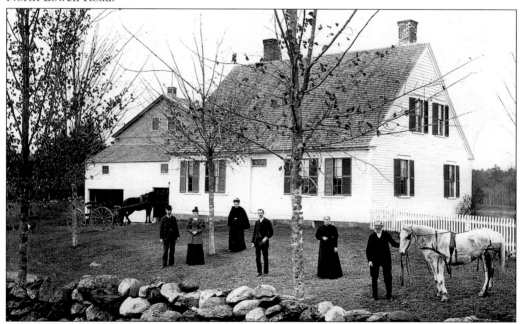

In 1805, the Reverend Samuel Harris was called to preach at the Presbyterian church. He built this house in 1811. Pictured, from left to right, are John Worledge, Ella (Harris) Worledge, Sally (Harris) Cault, William S. Harris, Philena (Dinsmoor) Harris, and William Harris. William S. Harris wrote a column in the *Exeter Newsletter* from 1880 to 1917, providing much of what we know about Windham's past. This house was torn down and replaced by a shopping center on Indian Rock Road.

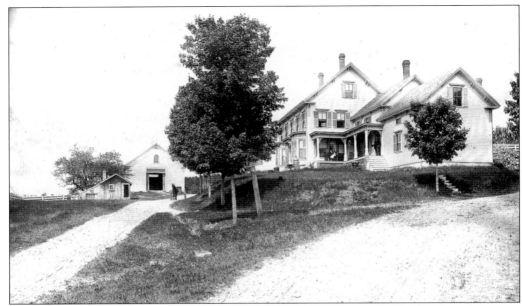

The John H. Dinsmore farm was once located at the intersection of Indian Rock and Country Roads. This impressive Victorian home replaced an older house in 1887. This farm was part of the 1,400 acres running from Jenny's Hill to Cobbett's Pond that was granted to the Dinsmoor family in 1741. Robert Frost worked here as a farm hand in the summer of 1891. In the above photograph, John Dinsmore and his wife, Adrianna, are on the porch with their infant son, George. John Dinsmore is pictured below with one of his horses. Interstate 93 divided the farm in the 1960s, and the house burned later.

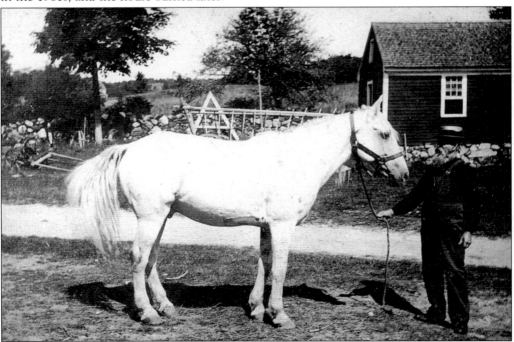

Three
THE RANGE AND
SOUTH WINDHAM

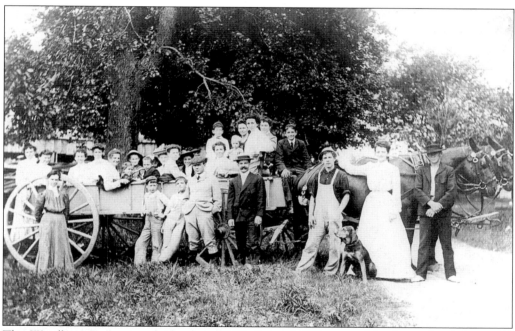

The Windham Range was laid out in 1728. Some 1,200 acres of land was divided into 20 parcels, which were long and narrow and ran between the shores of Cobbett's Pond and Canobie Lake. In this photograph from 1900, George Johnson stands in the center with a wagonload of summer boarders on Range Road. Chester Johnson wears the overalls and hat, and his younger brother, Irving, stands to the far right in front of the horses. Wagons like this carried boarders to outings or dances at Granite State Grove or Canobie Lake Park.

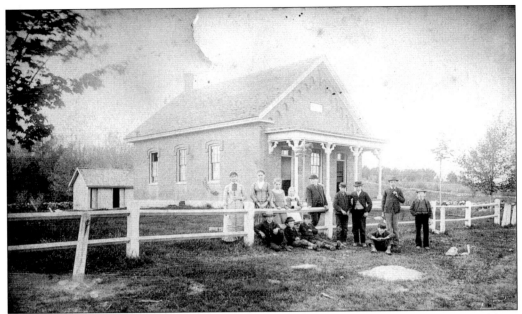

The students of the No. 1 Schoolhouse and their teachers pose for photographer Baldwin Coolidge. Students identified include Jamie L. Dinsmoor, Everett Hanson, Elmer Cochran, Alice Haseltine, William Hanson, and Fred Hunnewell. Edward Searles later enclosed this school within the walls of his estate. (Courtesy of the Nesmith Library.)

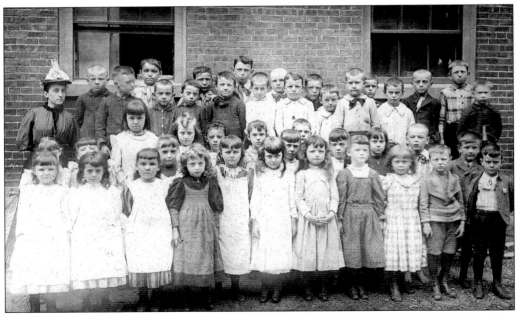

This very early photograph depicts a large group of children from the No. 1 Schoolhouse. Not a smile graces any of the faces. One teacher supervises 43 children.

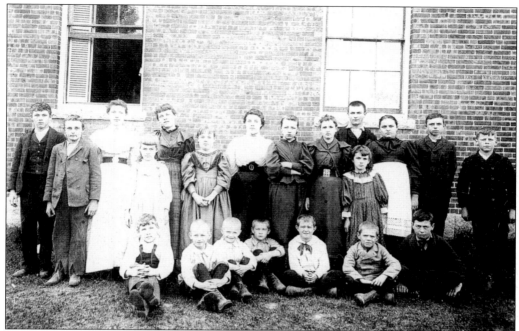

The children of the No. 1 Schoolhouse pose for a photograph with their teacher in 1892. Some of the children include, from left to right, the following: (front row) Chester Johnson (age nine, first) and Irving Johnson (age 6, fourth); (back row) Alta Johnson (age 12, fifth) and George Dinsmore Sr. (age 10, last). The teachers and other children are unidentified.

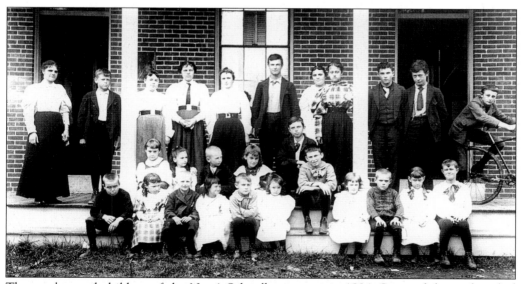

The teacher and children of the No. 1 Schoolhouse pose in 1894. Some of those identified include, from left to right, the following: (front row) Irving Johnson (age 8, fifth) and Edna Johnson (age 6, ninth); (back row) George Dinsmore Sr. (age 12, second) and Alta Johnson (age 14, fourth). There is a great bike on the far right.

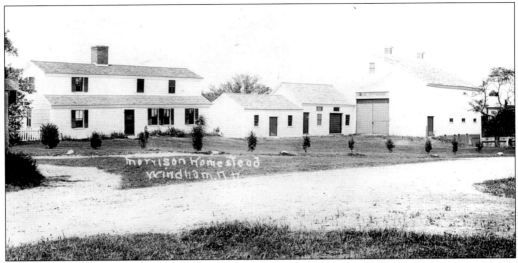

This farm was laid out to James Morrison as part of the Range in 1728. His son Samuel built this house *c.* 1730. Samuel was a lieutenant in the French and Indian War who was noted for his piety and was a leading man in town. Leonard Morrison said, "In this house have been many scenes of exuberant mirth and the deepest sadness. . . . Generations have gone with all they loved, with hopes both fulfilled and unfulfilled, and are almost forgotten; but the gambrel-roofed house stands." The house was torn down in the 1950s in order to widen Route 111.

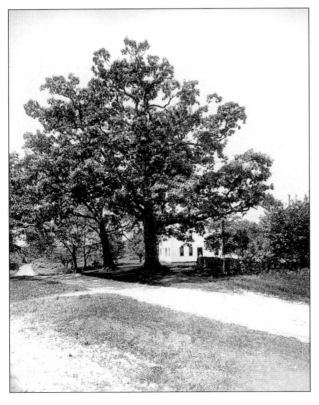

Robert Park built this house in 1742, and members of the Park family continued to occupy the property until 1940. His son Capt. Joseph Park followed him on the farm and operated a cider mill. He also sold cordwood in Haverhill and rafted it down the Merrimack to Newburyport. Joseph married Mary Dinsmoor, and they had nine children together. Their son, also named Joseph Park, returned to the farm after becoming a mason in Haverhill. He married Charena Cochran, and she bore six children. John A. Park and his sister Mary Ellen never married and were the last of the Parks to occupy the property.

Alexander Park originally owned this farm. He was a blacksmith by trade and met his wife, Sarah Maxwell, when she was thrown from her horse and broke her arm in front of his house. They married and had five daughters. Robert Armstrong married their daughter Alice. Since the Parks had no sons, they adopted Robert as their own. He built this home (pictured in the early 1800s) to replace the older house. In 1884, George F. Armstrong built a large Victorian home on the property. The farm was passed down through the generations and remained in the Armstrong family until 1957. This photograph shows the barnyard of the old Armstrong house after a snowstorm. The barn now houses the Common Man Restaurant.

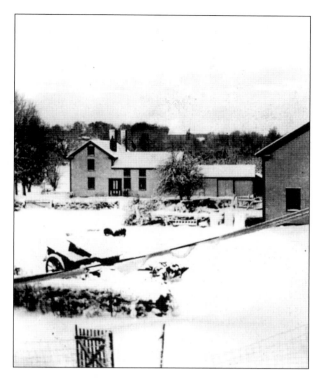

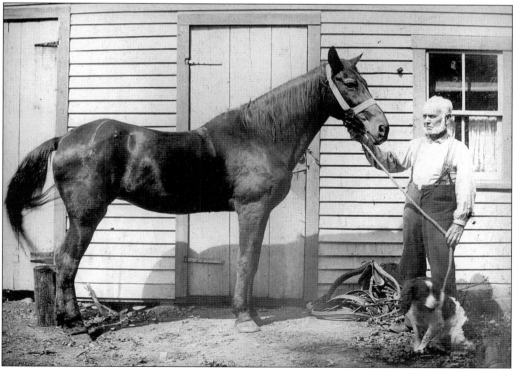

John A. Park is shown with his horse and dog in front of his farm on Range Road.

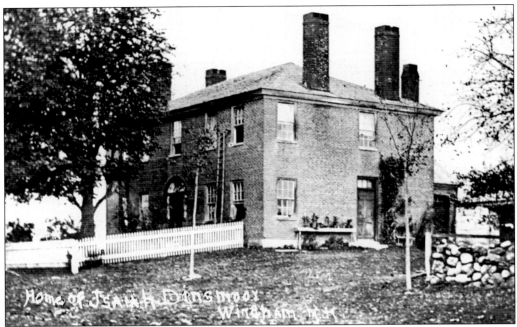

Home of Isaiah Dinsmoor Windham N.H.

Thomas Morrison was the first to settle here in 1729. The brick house was built in 1812 by Col. Alexander Park, who operated a blacksmith shop on the property. Isaiah Dinsmoor purchased the property in 1857. His wife's paternal grandfather, Andrew Park, had once owned the farm. Mary (Park) Dinsmoor was a teacher and contributed articles to the *Youth's Companion* and other periodicals. Their son Horace Park Dinsmoor followed them here on the farm. The photograph above shows the Federal-style house as it was originally built, with four chimneys. In 1901, Edward Wright, a jobber from Lawrence, Massachusetts, purchased the property and completed extensive renovations. He replaced the fireplaces and added the mansard roof. Edward Searles then purchased the property and enclosed it with wire fencing, as seen below.

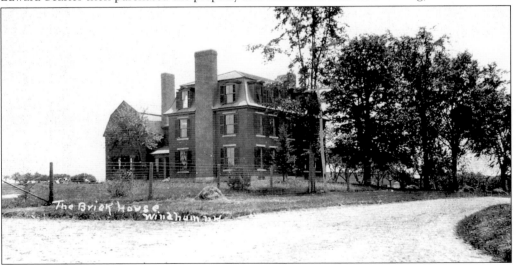

The Brick House Windham N.H.

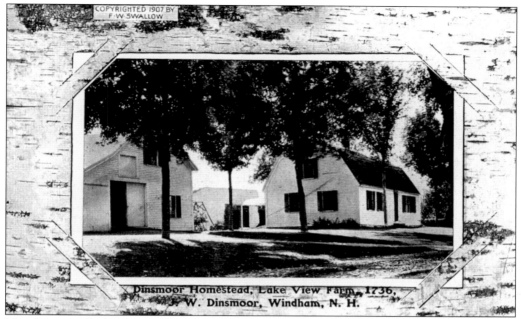

Dinsmoor Homestead, Lake View Farm, 1736.
W. Dinsmoor, Windham, N. H.

This farm was laid out to William Humphrey in 1728, and John Dinsmoor Jr. purchased the property in 1830. He and a neighbor, the Reverend Jacob Abbot, were faithful members of the Unitarian Society. On November 2, 1834, both drowned after attending a Unitarian meeting at town hall, when their leaky, old boat sank while they attempted to cross Cobbett's Pond. He left his wife and one-year-old son, Joseph, who later turned the farm into a productive orchard and vineyard.

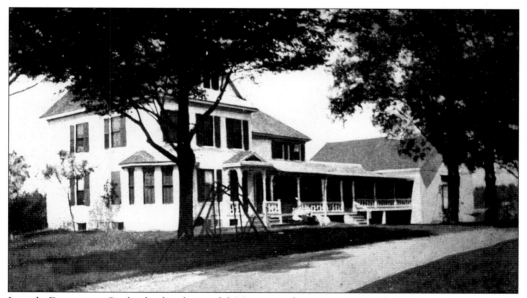

Joseph Dinsmoor Sr. built this beautiful Victorian home in 1884. Carrie B. Dinsmoor later operated a boardinghouse here known as Lake View House. When Joseph Dinsmoor Jr. took over the farm, he tore out all of his father's orchards and vineyards in order to grow hay.

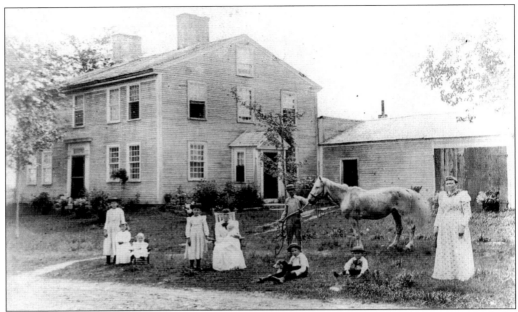

This house was built *c.* 1753 by Deacon Gavin Armor. George W. Johnson purchased the property in 1884, and this photograph of his family was taken *c.* 1891. From left to right are Alta Johnson, Forest Belyea, Helen Belyea, Ethel Belyea, Addie Belyea (with her baby Edmund), George W. Johnson (holding the horse), Chester Johnson, Irving Johnson, and Lizzie Johnson.

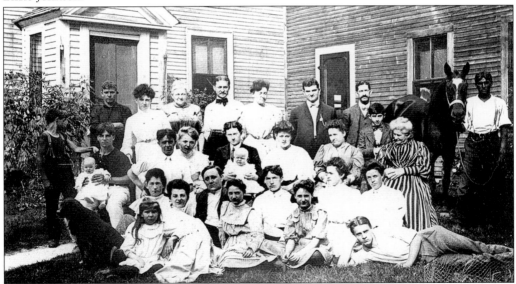

Boarders staying at Highland View Farm pose with members of the Johnson family. Mildred Johnson appears in the front row, leaning against Ann Johnson. Bill Smith is in the second row, holding baby Elfreda. Baby Wilfred Johnson is in the second row, sitting on the lap of Frank Miers. The back row includes, from left to right, Chester Johnson, Edna Johnson Smith, Lizzie Johnson, Ralph Smith, Myrtle Rich, and two unidentified men. Irving Johnson is standing, as always, with his horse.

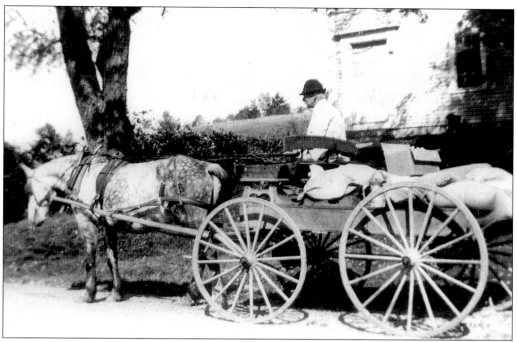

George Johnson heads out on his milk route. Metal cans filled with milk are stowed in the back of the wagon and are ready to be delivered to folks around town.

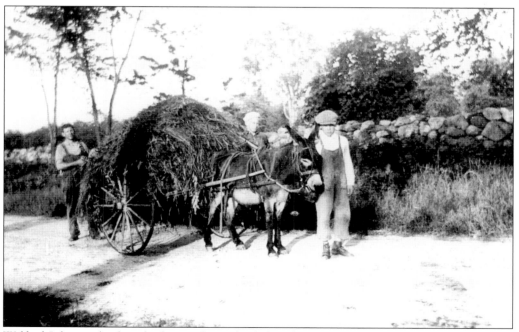

Wilfred Johnson leads a donkey and cart loaded with hay up Range Road. Chester Johnson follows behind the cart. The third person is unidentified.

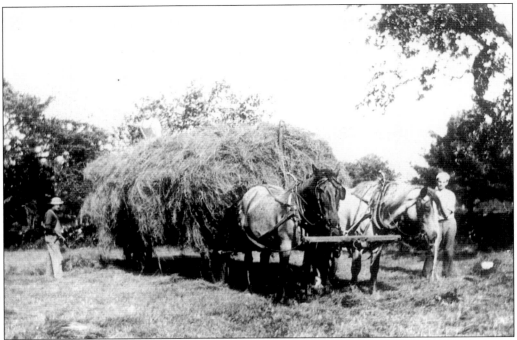

Taken at the beginning of the 20th century, this photograph shows a team of horses bringing in the hay at Highland View Farm, a summer ritual on farms all over Windham.

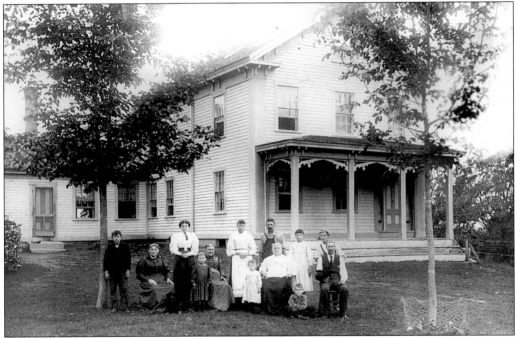

Mrs. J.V. Constantineau owned this farm in the 1890s. In the 20th century, it was home to Fred Sawyer. Some members of the Johnson family pose in front of the house, which is still standing across the street from Highland View Farm.

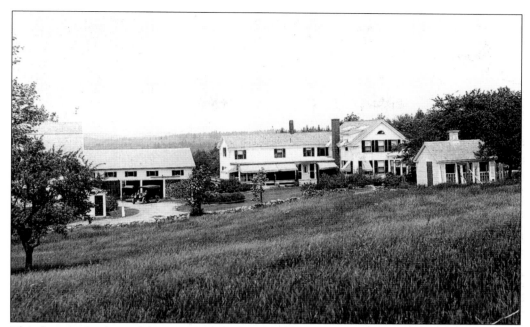

This farm had a beautiful setting overlooking Cobbett's Pond. John Hall built the house in 1842, and the Simpson family owned the property for a number of years. The land extended to the shore of Cobbett's Pond, where "Long Albert" Simpson started Sycamore Grove in 1894. The property was sold to Julia Baker in 1909, and then John Mackenzie operated the Windham Auto Inn here from 1934 to 1947. Notice the lovely automobile in the driveway.

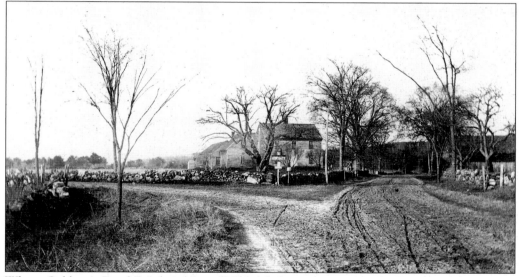

Where Cobbett's Pond Road and Lowell Road fork was known as "the Parting of the Ways." Rev. Calvin Cutler built the house shown in 1839. Reverend Cutler was an active abolitionist and the minister in Windham from 1828 until 1844. He replaced an existing house that had once been owned by the Reverend Simon Williams. Williams was a beloved minister and celebrated teacher at his private academy. Later, M.E. Call operated her popular boardinghouse Elm Farm here.

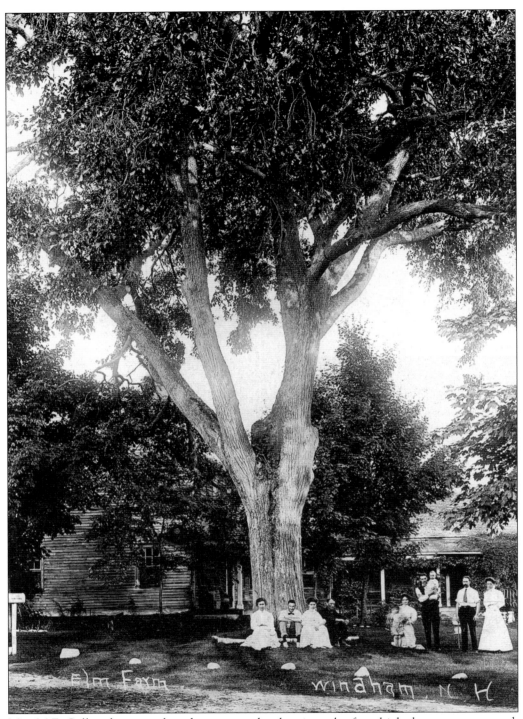

Mrs. M.E. Call and summer boarders pose under the giant elm for which the spot was named. Call opened Elm Farm Hall on August 19, 1899, with a special concert at 7:45, fireworks at 9:30, and dancing from 10 until midnight.

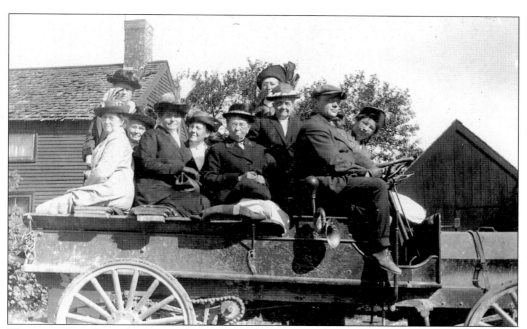

These teachers from the Dover Street School in Lowell, Massachusetts, head to their annual outing. The photograph was taken in front of the Red House on Cobbett's Pond Road.

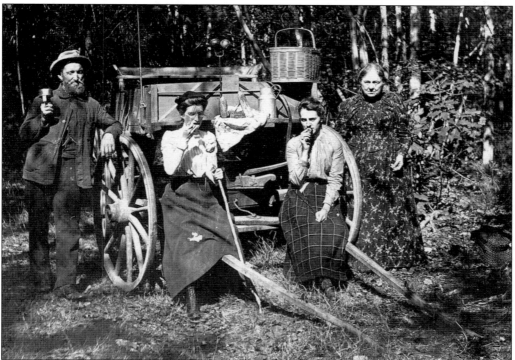

John Dalton Warren (left, with the cover to the metal jug) and his wife, Sophia (far right), enjoy a picnic in Windham with two unidentified women sitting on the wagon. They are eating roasted corn.

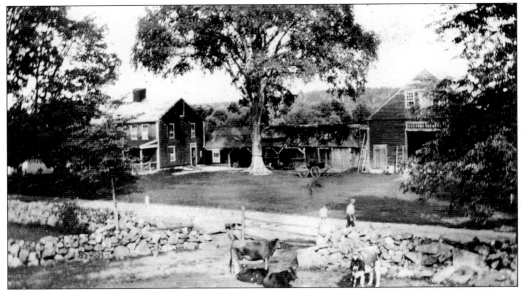

This house was likely built in 1775, since a foundation stone is inscribed with that date. Moses Noyes, a veteran of the Revolutionary War, built the house, and it was passed down through his family until 1881. His descendant James Noyes quipped, "I have worn these stones smaller, digging them to plant my corn and potatoes," which was a common complaint of Windham farmers. Peter A. Zins purchased the property in 1917. He ran a dairy farm and also raised vegetables to sell to the summer residents on Cobbett's Pond.

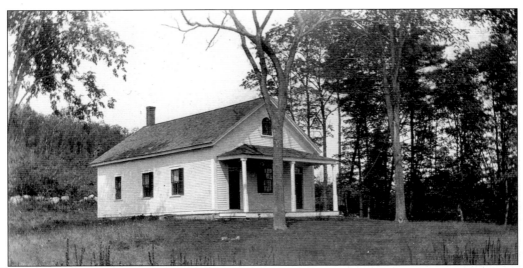

The No. 2 Schoolhouse was located on Range Road between Cobbett's Pond and Golden Brook Road. This was the fourth schoolhouse to serve the district that was known as "the Row" in early times. James W. Smith, a native of the district, was the architect and builder. The cost was $1,400. The Reverend Loren Thayer dedicated the building on December 8, 1853, and the town sold the building to William and Gertrude Hazlett in the 1940s. It was torn down later.

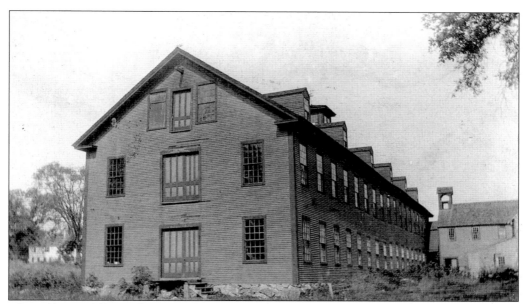

The mill in South Windham was the only large factory ever to be built in town. The first grant of water rights to Cobbett's Pond was given to Samuel Senter for a gristmill. In 1833, Isaac Senter sold the mill to the father of Stephen Fessenden of Boston. He moved here and first built a shingle and clapboard mill. A building for carding rolls, enlarged to produce twilled flannel and frocking, followed this. In 1870, the property was sold to George S. Neal, who sought and received a seven-year tax break as an inducement for building a larger mill. The mill building pictured was built in 1871. Neal continued to manufacture cloth here until the late 1890s. Edwin Stickney acquired the property through foreclosure proceedings and soon after sold the property to the Gould brothers, who manufactured witch hazel here until c. 1916. The buildings were torn down in the summer of 1920. In the photograph above, the size of the buildings is appreciated. Below, Golden Brook Road runs past the front of the mill.

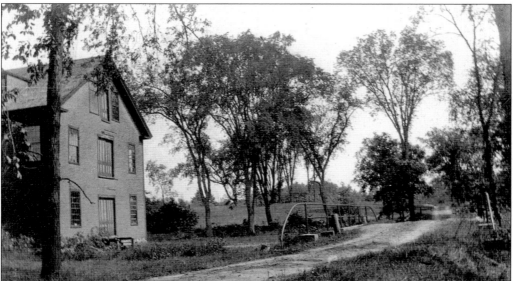

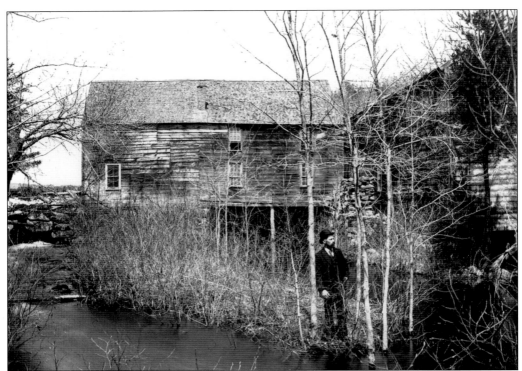

This photograph, taken in 1898, gives a rare glimpse of Simpson's Mill. Joseph Simpson, a fine carpenter and millwright, built the mill in 1789. Thomas W. Simpson, who was of no relation to Joseph, operated a gristmill, sawmill, and lumbermill here for much of the 19th century.

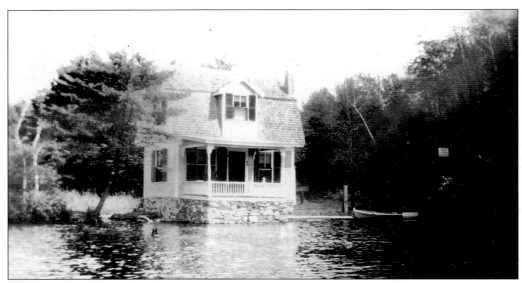

The Harry Simpson cottage on Rock Pond is shown as it appeared in 1929. Simpson owned all of the property on the southeast shore, including Deer Leap, and was a direct descendant of Capt. John Simpson, who was wounded on Bunker Hill in 1775. This charming Victorian cottage was built right out over the water. At the time, Rock Pond was a very secluded place.

Four
WINDHAM JUNCTION

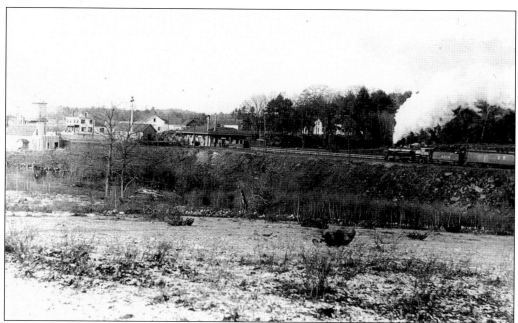

In this picture of Windham Junction in 1920, a northbound Manchester & Lawrence branch train slows to a stop at the station. The Manchester & Lawrence Railroad was constructed through Windham from 1848 to 1849. The first train operated on the line on November 13, 1849. As time passed, the railroads transformed Windham in many ways.

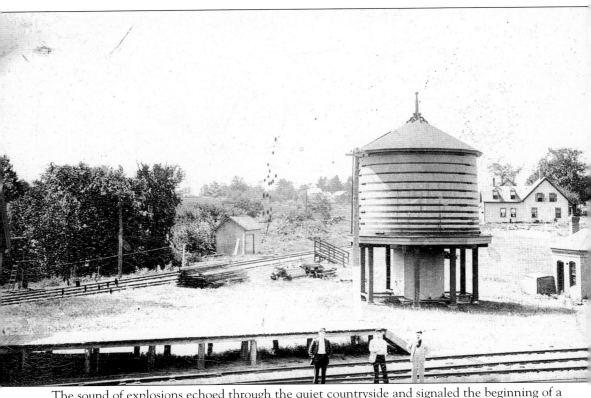

The sound of explosions echoed through the quiet countryside and signaled the beginning of a new era in Windham's history. The year was 1848, and the railroad bed was being cut through Windham's infamous ledge with black powder, hand tools, and the backs of the Irish immigrants. With the beginning of rail service in 1849 on the Manchester & Lawrence Railroad, Windham suddenly became an easy place to reach from the nearby industrial cities. Construction began on the Nashua & Rochester Railroad in 1873, and the first train operated on that line on November 24, 1874. These two lines met at what became Windham Junction. The crossing occurred about 375 feet south of the Manchester & Lawrence Railroad's Windham Station. The Nashua & Rochester Railroad erected a new station at the cost of $2,200. The old station was moved onto Depot Road and became known as the Railroad House.

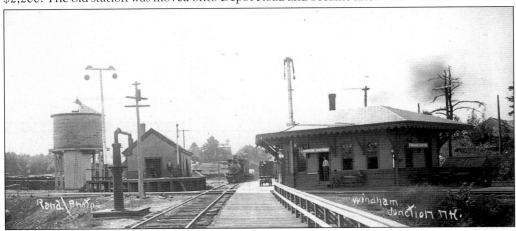

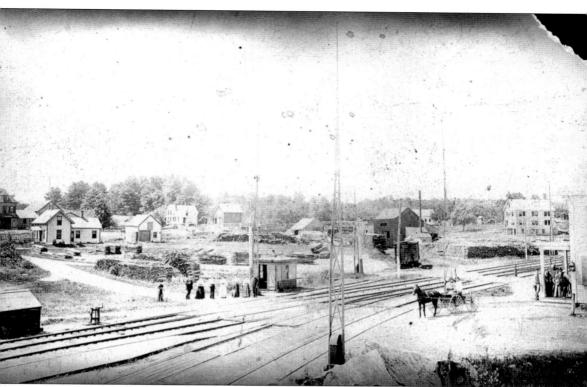

The panoramic view of Windham Junction above was photographed *c.* 1900. Piles of wood are destined to be shipped by rail out of town or will go to Seavey's Mill to be planed into boards. A crowd has gathered on the porch of the general store that is shown at the far right. The former station, known as the Railroad House, can be seen at the center on Depot Road, and behind it is the impressive Victorian home of George Seavey. The crossing attendant's house is near the crossing gates. To the left side of the photograph, the large water tank appears. A brick pump house next to the tank housed a small steam engine that powered the water pump, pumping water from a nearby well. The passenger station is shown in the two photographs below. The freight house is located on a raised platform across the tracks. Crossing protection at the Junction was provided by ball signals on the towers.

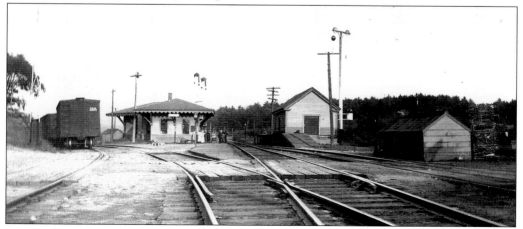

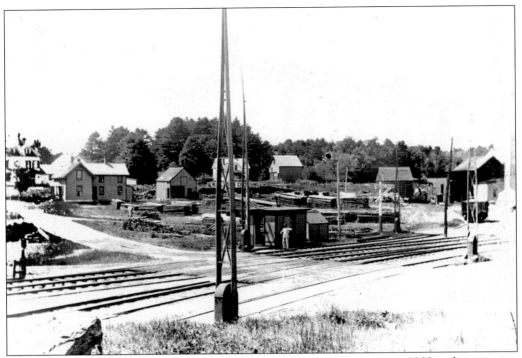

The Bar Harbor Express passed through Windham each summer starting in 1902 and continuing until 1911. Local people woke up their children early in the morning and took them here to watch the train with the famous millionaires pass by. Above is a later view of the Junction.

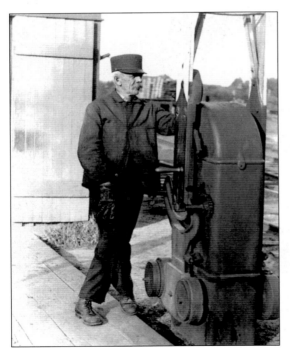

Many jobs were available in the Junction because of the railroads. Horace Boyce was a crossing attendant for a number of years, manually operating the gates. In the late 1800s, the shoe industry became interested in building factories near the Junction. However, some influential Windham residents did not like the idea and put pressure on the landowners not to sell. The businessmen moved on and built their shoe factories in Derry, changing the character of that town in many ways.

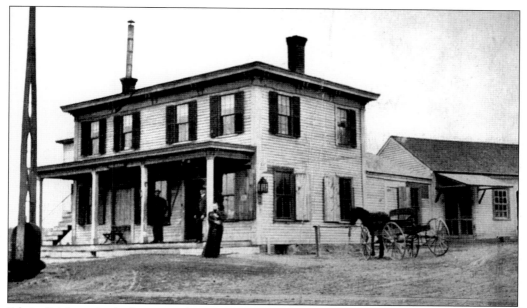

Edwin Stickney built this general store in 1861. The post office was located here, and a grain store operated out back. The store was the social center where local folks gossiped or caught up with the latest news and where neighborhood dances took place. E.W. Armstrong was the proprietor at the time of this photograph. The store burned in 1927.

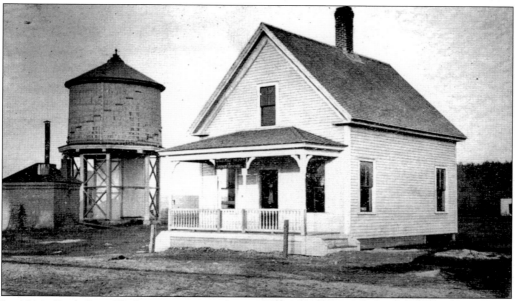

In 1911, Paul Otis Clyde was appointed postmaster of Windham and built this post office building on railroad-owned land near the water tank. In 1927, the general store and the attached building were destroyed in a spectacular fire. After the fire, Clyde began selling groceries from the post office and later added gasoline pumps. He remained the postmaster until 1945. At his retirement, the store closed and was finally torn down in 1965.

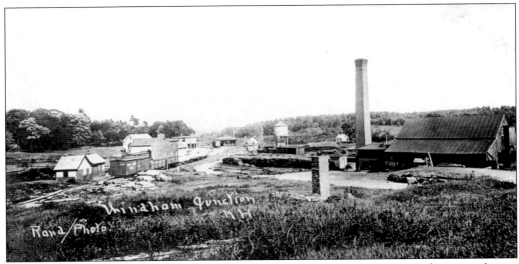

George Seavey was one of Windham's most prominent businessmen who owned vast timberland and engaged in several businesses. In 1865, Seavey built his first steam sawmill here with partners Hemphill Clark and John S. Brown. In 1877, Seavey enlarged and rebuilt the mill, adding cider presses and tanks. Normally six to eight men worked in the yard, with more in the winter, while as many as 50 horses were employed in hauling wood. The mill planed one million feet of board annually. Two hydraulic presses turned out 300 barrels of cider in 10 hours. More than 4,000 barrels of cider were made annually, with the majority sold to be manufactured into vinegar. The 65-foot chimney was a local landmark.

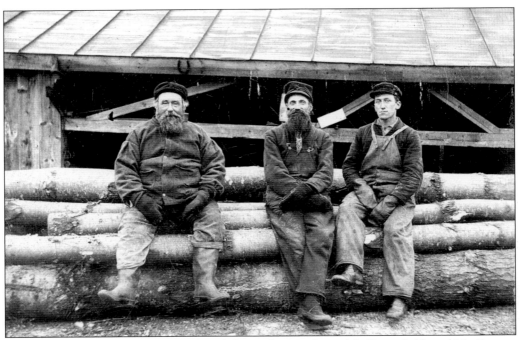

These workers at Seavey's Mill are, from left to right, Mr. Scott, Mr. Butterfield, and Mr. Easton.

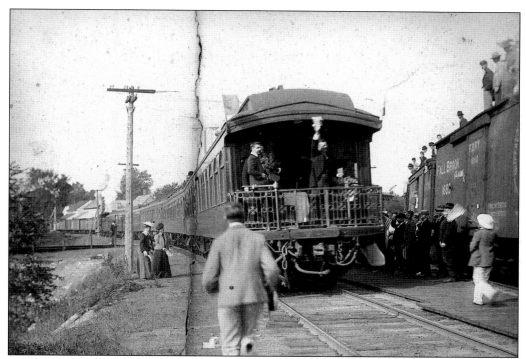

Pres. Theodore Roosevelt is shown on the whistle-stop tour that passed through Windham Junction during the 1904 campaign. A young boy chases after the train, waving an American flag.

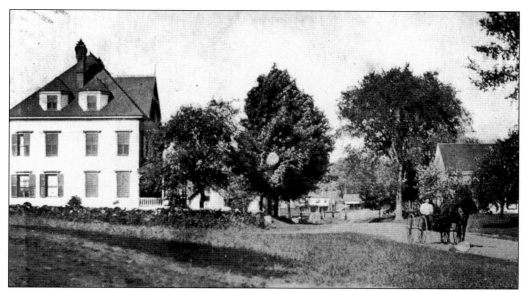

This old postcard reads, "Main Street looking east in Windham, N.H." George Seavey's stately Victorian home is featured prominently in the foreground.

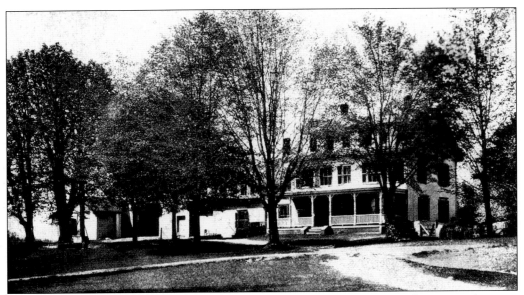

Maple Lawn Farm was a boardinghouse located near Windham Junction. This postcard view is interesting because it shows the third story, which was added to accommodate more guests. The farm was within easy walking distance of the railroad station.

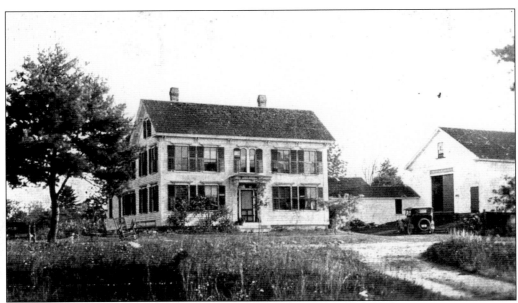

John Hughes was the first member of his family to own this farm. Legend says that he was a British soldier who deserted and then joined the American patriots fighting for independence. He moved to Windham after the war. Benjamin Hughes demolished the original house and built this one in 1876, and Horace Berry bought it in 1910. At the time of this postcard photograph, George H. Butterfield owned the property. It still stands on Morrison Road.

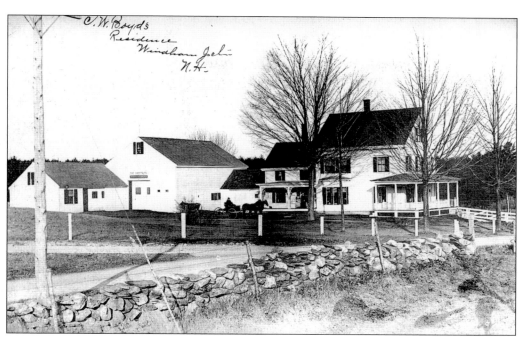

George W. Hughes built this house in the 1870s. He was a station agent at the Junction for many years. In this photograph, then owner C.W. Boyd sits in his carriage with a team attached. The house is still standing on North Lowell Road.

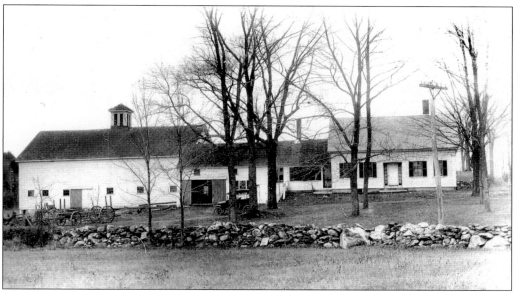

This was the home of Horace Berry, who married Harriet Hughes in 1867. When she died later in life, he married her sister Margaret. He and his second wife were activists and early environmentalists who strongly supported the Society for the Protection of New Hampshire Forests. They gave Garaphelia Park, near the Cemetery on the Plain, to the town. The plaque there reads, "The woodlands were gay and beautiful, for nature had clothed them in all her surpassing loveliness."

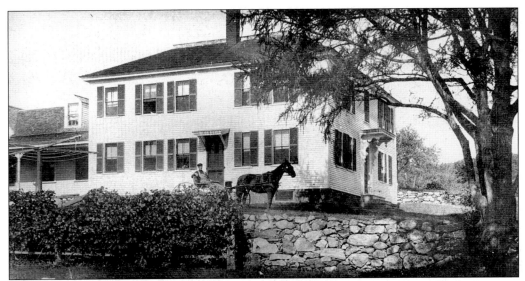

Peter Duston purchased this farm from Lt. Abraham Reid for 390 pounds in 1785. He was a soldier in the Revolutionary War and was known as a witty and impulsive character. His son Moses built this Federal-style home in the early 1800s. The farm was passed down to Moses's daughter Mary, who wed Nathaniel Ripley. After 1870, the property passed through a number of owners. For many years, it was a large and productive farm known as the Northland.

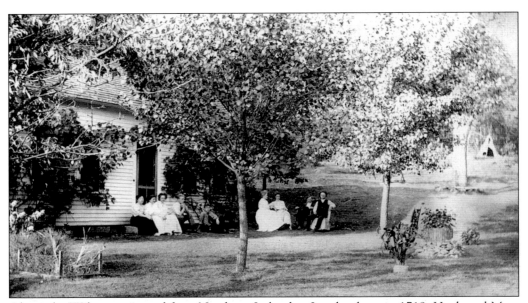

Alexander Wilson emigrated from Northern Ireland to Londonderry in 1719. Hugh and Mary Ann (Cochran) Wilson were the first of the Wilson family to occupy this farm. Hugh purchased it from Dr. Moody Morse in 1801. The house sits on the Windham-Derry line, but since the doorway is in Windham, the Wilsons are considered residents of the town. Members of the family have lived in this house for more than 200 years. Pictured here with several boarders are Clarence Wilson (fourth from the left); Harvey Wilson (fifth); their mother, Mary Wilson (sixth); and their father, Aaron Wilson (eighth).

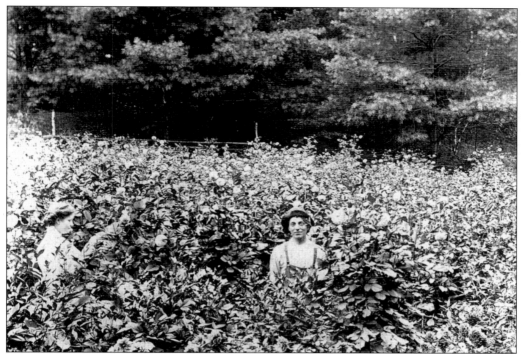

Della Lundberg and Willard Clyde are shown in Clyde's impressive dahlia garden.

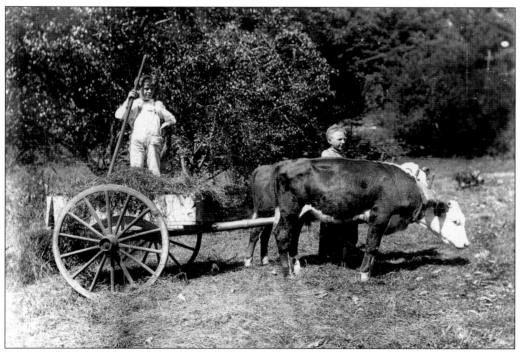

Harvey Wilson (left) and his brother Clarence gather hay with a wagon pulled by two young heifers.

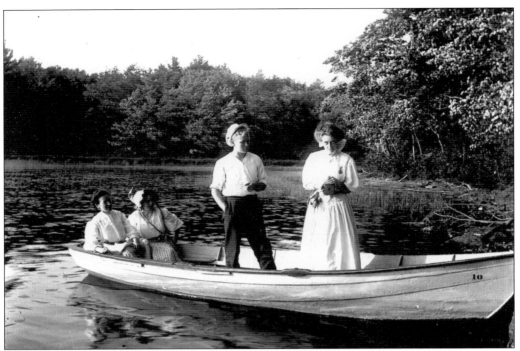

Clarence Wilson takes summer boarders boating at Mitchell's Pond.

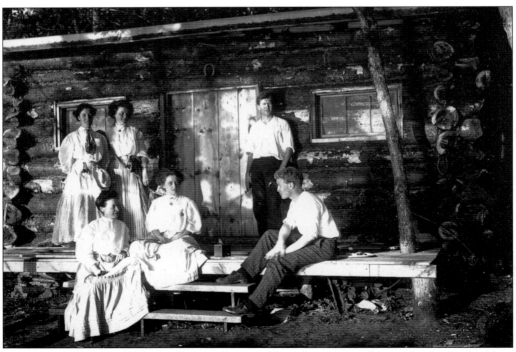

Harvey and Clarence Wilson, along with several boarders, sit on the porch of a log building that was once part of the infamous Bissell's Camp near Mitchell's Pond.

Five
WEST WINDHAM

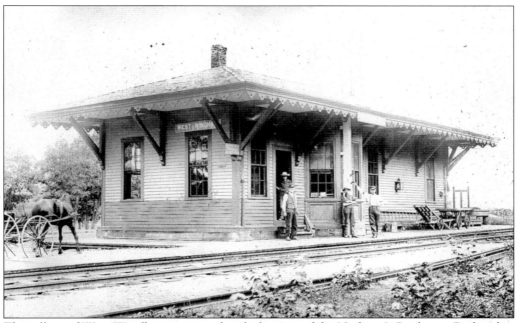

The village of West Windham prospered with the start of the Nashua & Rochester Railroad in 1874. Pictured at West Windham Station are, from left to right, Joseph Crowell, Al Farmer, and Frank Crowell. After a train accident in 1907, it was renamed Anderson Station to avoid confusion with Windham Junction. Train service ended here in 1934.

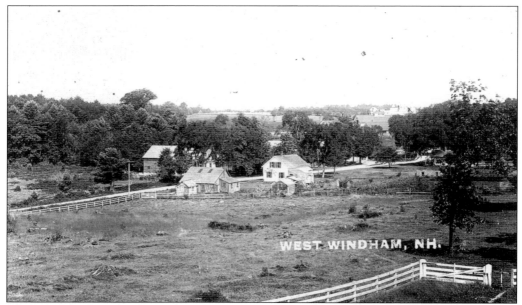

This panoramic view of West Windham shows the well-tended farms along Mammoth Road. The farms on the hill in the distance are in Londonderry. Many of the people there took a West Windham address because of the post office and social life in the village.

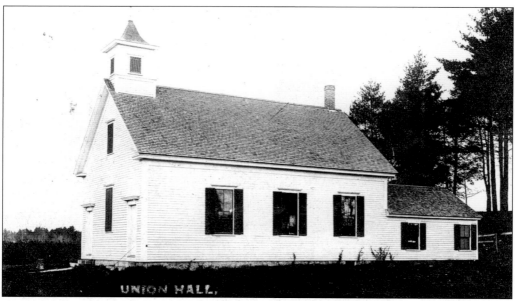

West Windham was a growing place, and the residents felt they should have a hall in which to meet for literary, social, and religious purposes. In 1880, Union Hall was built for $650, the money raised with the sale of $5 shares. The building measured 32 by 26 feet and was fitted inside with a large hall with a low stage and a kitchen. Over the years, many religious and social functions have been held here. Dancing was banned in 1881 but became popular later.

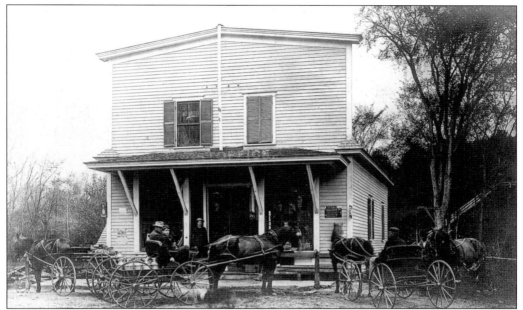

Neighbors gather in front of the store and post office in West Windham. Bartley & Underhill built the first store here in 1838. The original store burned in January 1901. George Clark was the proprietor at the time and lost everything with the exception of the mail. The fire started from the stove, and Clark's residence next door was nearly lost. A new store and post office was built and, at the time of this photograph, was run by Mr. Emerson. His neighbor Mr. Andrews ran a blacksmith shop.

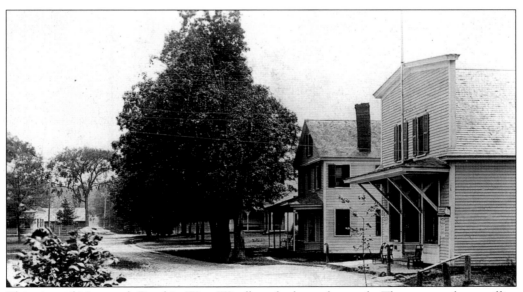

This view of Mammoth Road in West Windham looks to the south. The store and post office can be seen in the foreground on the right. Note the chairs and hitching post out front.

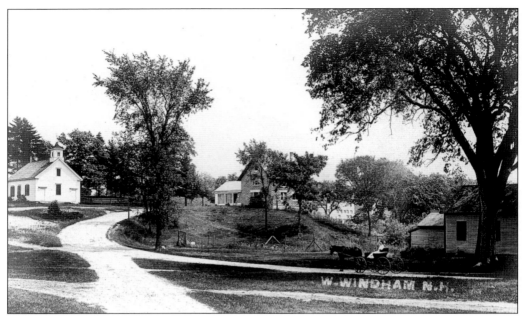

Union Hall sits on the hill watching over this quiet scene in West Windham. The unique, pressed-cement-block house had recently been built across the street. In the foreground, a young lady sits in her horse-drawn buggy.

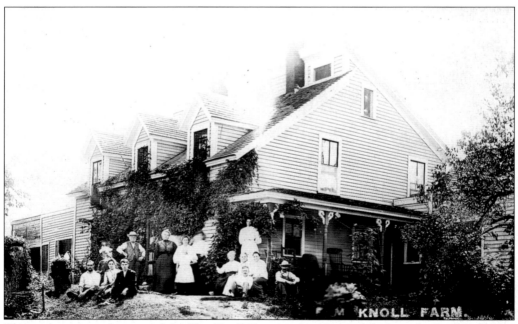

The proprietors and guests of the Elm Knoll Farm pose in front of this popular boardinghouse in West Windham. Several boardinghouses like this one were located along Kendall Pond Road. Brookside Farm was a three-story boardinghouse with 30 rooms. Dozens of boardinghouses operated in Windham at the beginning of the 20th century.

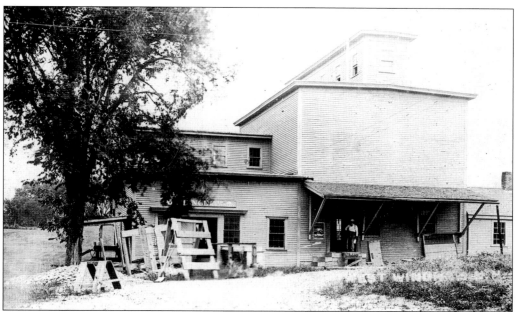

Henry Campbell built the first mill at this location in 1750. John A. Burnham built a 40- by 60-foot factory here in 1836. In good times, Burnham manufactured 4,000 yards of "satinet" cloth a month. In 1837, a depression hit, and his firm failed because of the heavy debts from the construction of the mill. Beginning in 1845, Ira Hersey manufactured worsted yarn here. Edward Titcomb, a merchant from Newburyport, Massachusetts, purchased the mill in 1848 and produced mattresses. The mill and $600 worth of lumber burned in 1857. The mill was rebuilt and operated as a grain and gristmill by Walter Drucker. This building also burned. William Anderson constructed the mill and dam shown in these photographs c. 1900. This mill was also operated as a grain and gristmill and was managed first by Mr. Andrews and later by Walton Barker.

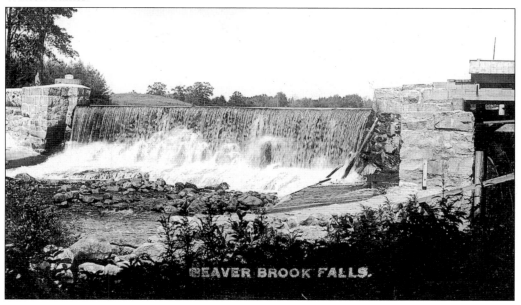

BEAVER BROOK FALLS.

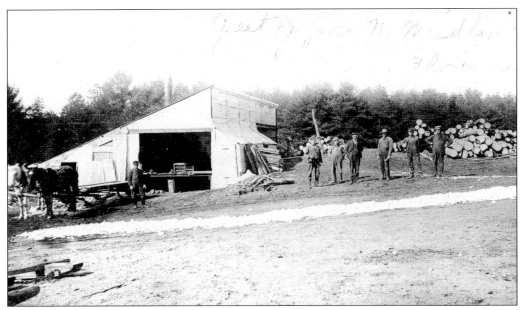

This steam sawmill operated in West Windham c. 1907. These mills stripped valuable timber from the wood lots in town and sent it on to the neighboring cities. The men stand in front of piles of pine logs while the team of horses waits to pull more from the woods. Timber was a cash crop, and many farms had sawmills as part of their operations.

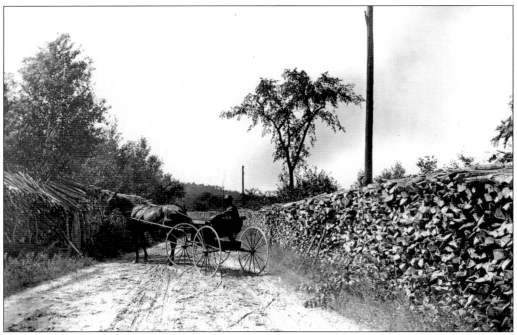

Wood is stacked along Mammoth Road as far as the eye can see. It is ready to be shipped out of town in this photograph from 1898. During the winter of 1910, more than 100 railroad cars a month were loaded with lumber and wood at West Windham Station.

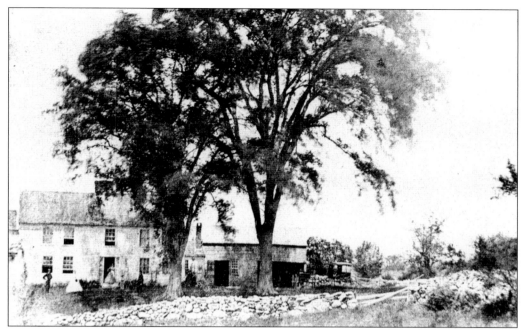

This very early photograph shows the original Campbell homestead. A beautiful saltbox Colonial, the building sat at a right angle to Kendall Pond Road so that the front of the house, with its bank of windows, faced south toward the winter sun. Henry and Martha (Black) Campbell were the first of the family to live here, purchasing 240 acres in 1733. Their son Deacon Samuel Campbell built the pictured house in 1756.

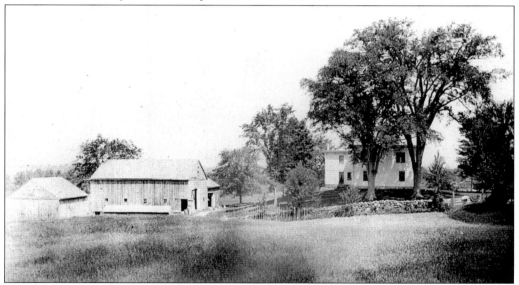

The second Deacon Samuel Campbell, the great-grandson of the first Deacon Campbell, tore down the first house in order to build a new one in 1868. It was built in the same location but with the front now facing Kendall Pond Road. The two elm trees remain standing, and the original barn can be seen behind the house. This farm is still one of the most beautiful places in town.

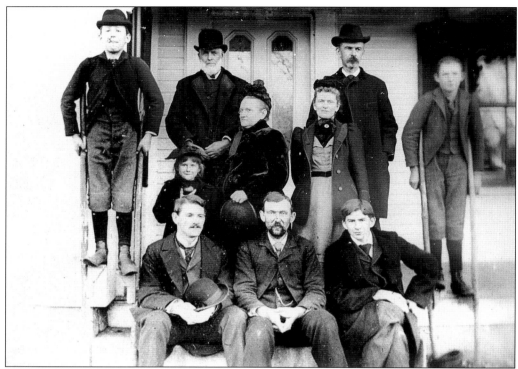

Members of the Campbell family pose *c.* 1890. From left to right are the following: (front row) Arthur; Alphonso; and Percy; (back row) Willis, on stilts; Samuel; his wife, Lydia; Alphonso's wife, Eliza; and young Sam, on stilts.

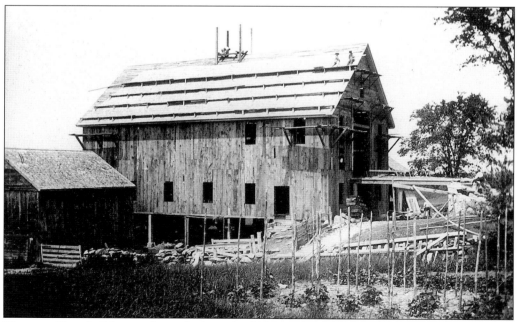

The new Campbell barn is being built in the 1890s with a bridge to the upper floor.

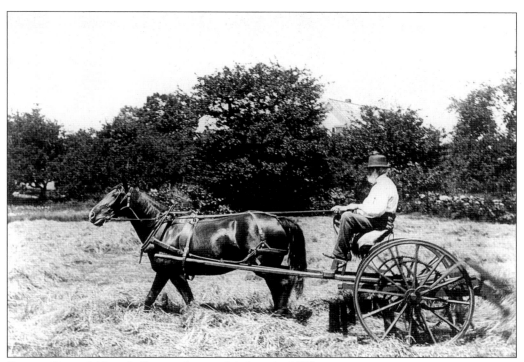
Deacon Samuel Campbell mows hay on his farm in 1895.

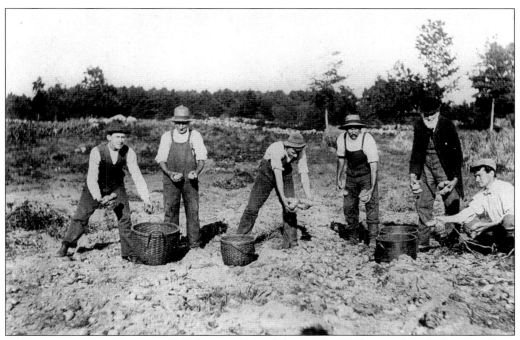
Digging potatoes on the Campbell farm are, from left to right, Willis, unidentified, young Sam, Alphonso, and Samuel. This c. 1895 photograph was taken in a field near Kendall Pond Road.

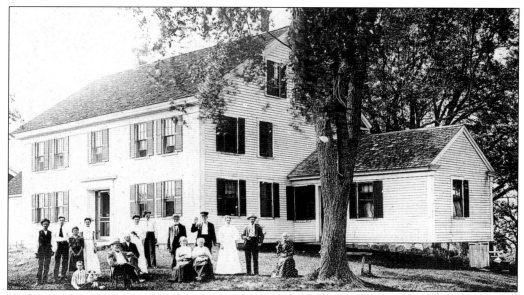

Herbert and Etta Russell are shown with summer boarders at Castle Hill Farm. Robert Jackson, a Boston architect and wealthy gentleman farmer, purchased this farm in 1915. He filled the house with a valuable collection of fine antiques. On January 17, 1931, the house burned along with $20,000 worth of antiques. The devastated Jackson had a nervous breakdown.

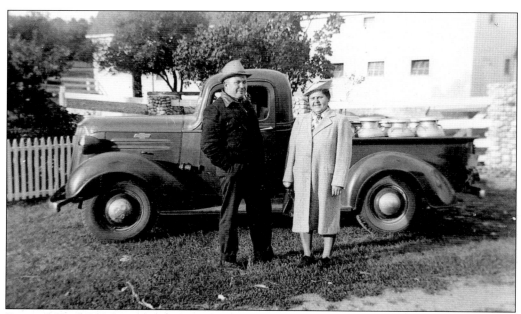

Ben and Josefa Markewich stand in front of their pickup truck loaded with milk cans ready to be delivered. Markewich ran a successful dairy farm with more than 65 cows. The photograph was taken at Castle Hill Farm in 1943.

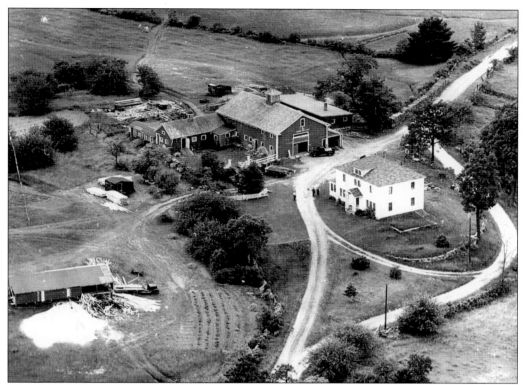

In 1917, Ben and Josefa Markewich purchased a small dairy farm next to Robert Jackson's on Castle Hill Road. They worked long, hard hours and, after the fire at Jackson's farm, had enough money saved to purchase his barn and land. A short time later, a fire destroyed their own home, garage, and all of their farm equipment. They lived for a short time in the shed next to the barn, until a new house could be built in 1933. This photograph shows the new house, the old barn, and a large sawmill in the foreground. It was taken prior to 1940.

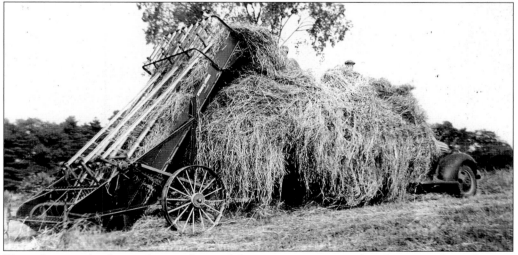

This photograph shows the mechanized haying practices employed on Castle Hill Farm in 1944.

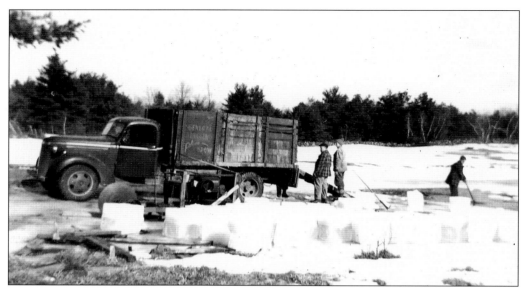

Men gather ice at Castle Hill Farm in 1944. Ice harvesting was an important part of rural life. The farmers harvested ice from ponds to keep their milk cold until it could be delivered. In the early days before electricity, ice was the only way to keep food cold. It was harvested off Cobbett's Pond, and a number of icehouses were located along the shore. These houses had walls filled with sawdust to prevent melting.

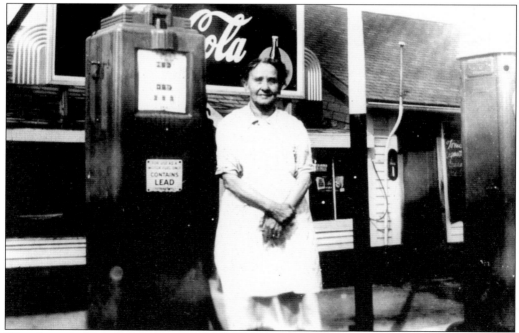

Waterhouse's Store has been a local landmark since 1921. Ethel Waterhouse first opened a roadside stand in 1921. Alice Waterhouse is shown here in front of the store in the 1930s.

Six

THE CANOBIE LAKE DISTRICT

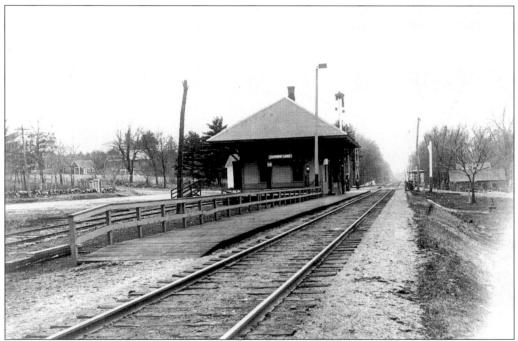

Leonard Morrison headed a group of Windham residents who petitioned the railroad commission to build a station closer to their homes and businesses. The request was granted and the station was built in 1885. The commissioners wanted a dignified name for the station. Morrison suggested Canobie Lake, a name taken from Cannonbie, Scotland, honoring the Scotch families living in Windham. It is a tribute to the power and influence of the railroad that the name of the nearby lake was changed from Policy Pond to Canobie Lake.

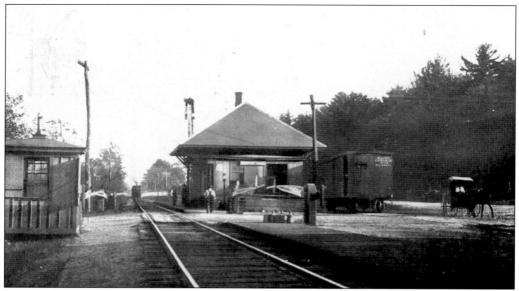

As in other villages in Windham, the area took the name of the post office at the railroad station. Homes and businesses were said to be located in Canobie Lake, New Hampshire. Following the opening of the station, a telegraph, telephone, and American Express office were opened. The busy station catered to the people living in the eastern part of Windham and opened Cobbett's Pond and Canobie Lake to development by making them accessible by train.

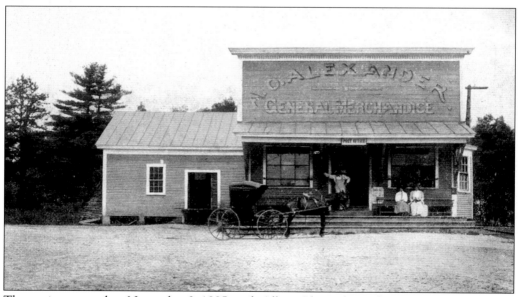

The station opened on November 9, 1885, with Albert Alexander as the station agent. He then started construction on a store nearby. The Canobie Lake Post Office was established here on February 26, 1886, with Alexander as the postmaster. In this view, he stands in the doorway of his store while two ladies sit on the front porch. He operated a dry goods, grocery, and general country store.

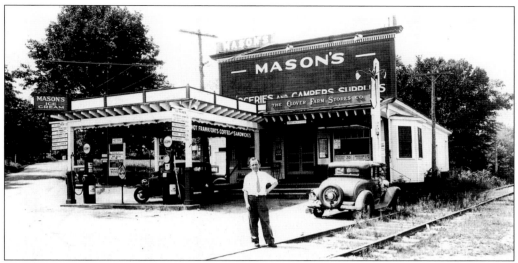

Bob Mason Sr. is shown above in front of his store at Canobie Lake Station in the early 1930s. The many signs advertise groceries, campers' supplies, and Mason's ice cream. A directional sign in the background advertises Hadley's Beach, Armstrong's Beach, the Lakeview Golf Course, and the Windham Auto Inn. As seen below, the store featured a lunch counter offering sandwiches, pies, and ice-cream treats. Granite State potato chips were dispensed from the glass container on the counter, and Hill's ice-old beverages are displayed in a vending machine. Mason's was a convenient stop for campers heading to Cobbett's or Canobie.

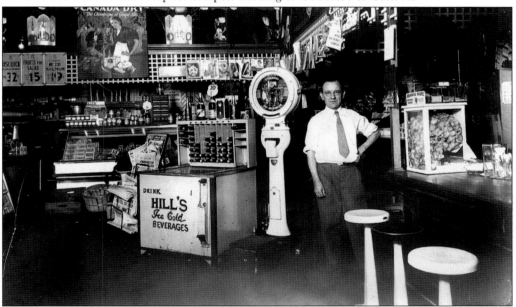

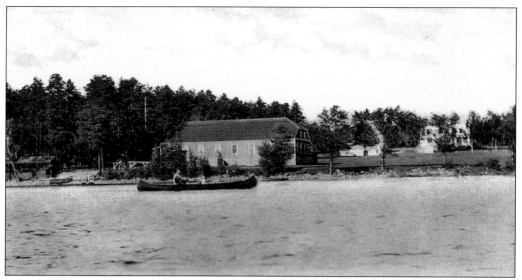

Pictured above in its heyday, the Granite State Grove was one of the most successful business enterprises in Windham. In 1850, Policy Pond Grove was opened to the public. The picnic groves and swimming were the main attractions. The property was sold to William Smith of Boston in 1867, and he set about adding stables and a bowling alley. Abel Dow purchased the property in 1877, changing the name to Granite State Grove. The new railroad station was a windfall for his business. The grove became a popular place for outings, with attractions including a shooting gallery and a roller-skating rink. There was an excellent restaurant, and nightlife centered on the dance hall. Of course, the main attractions remained the picnic groves, boats, and swimming. In 1902, the Massachusetts Northeastern Street Railway built Canobie Lake Park to increase the ridership on weekends. This was direct competition. In 1903, swimming was banned, and in 1909, a devastating fire destroyed most of the buildings. Below is a view of Canobie Lake from Granite State Grove.

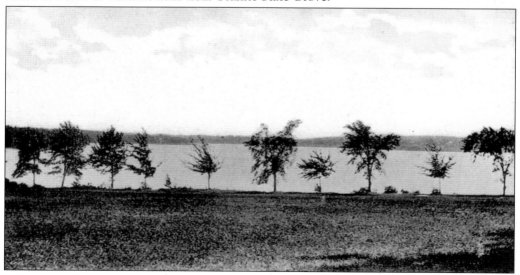

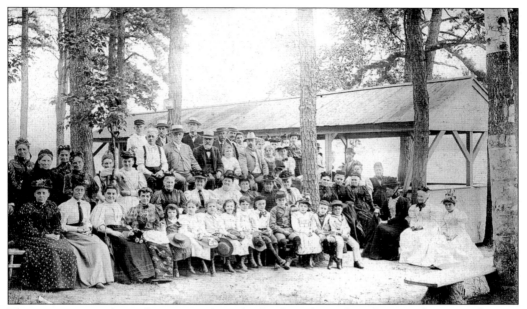

The grove attracted an eclectic mix of people. On Saturday nights, the grove became a dancing mecca, with the Peak Sisters and other headliners of the day appearing at the dance hall. On Sundays in 1897, the Reverend James Harper of the Presbyterian church led revival services at 4:00 p.m., followed by baptisms in the lake. The wonderful photograph shows a Sunday school picnic at the grove in 1900. The people are decked out in their finest clothes.

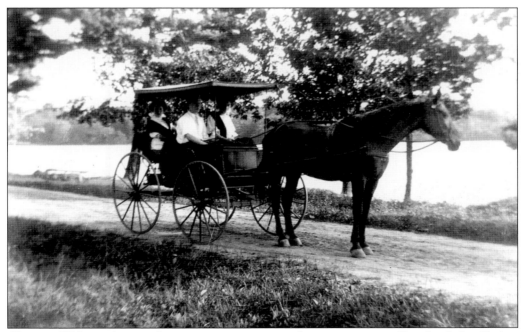

Clarence Wilson, along with two passengers, returns from an outing to Canobie Lake. He has stopped his handsome carriage on Policy Road at the Windham line.

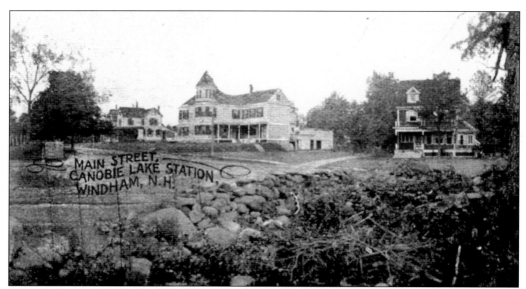

This old postcard view shows Main Street at Canobie Lake Station. Abel Dow built a private residence here in 1883, near his Granite State Grove, on Canobie Lake. Albert Alexander, the station agent and storekeeper, built a house here in 1888. William McElhinney and Edwin Dinsmoor both constructed houses in 1891. William Meserve purchased the Brown Mill on the turnpike in 1887 and built a home nearby in 1890. Meserve was a talented inventor who built one of the first automobiles in New Hampshire in 1896.

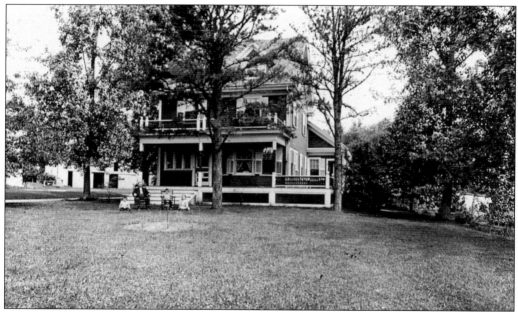

James Dinsmore built this house in the 1880s. Fred and Laura Webster lived here for a number of years, followed by their daughter Mildred Butterfield. The beautiful Victorian-era homes of the Canobie Lake district are landmarks still, indicating that motorists have passed over the line from Salem into Windham.

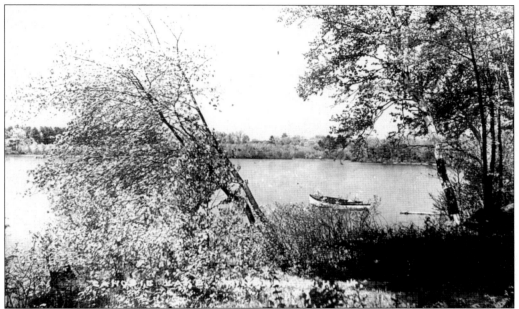

J.W. Dinsmoor and C.J. Miers built the first road to the shore of Canobie Lake in 1880 and sold camp lots. In 1903, Armstrong and Hall laid out fifty-two 50- by 100-foot lots on the shore. By 1906, most of the lots had been sold and 11 cottages had been built. No further development of the Windham shoreline occurred until the 1960s, when Windham Estates was subdivided. The view is from West Shore Road, looking toward what is Woodvue Road today.

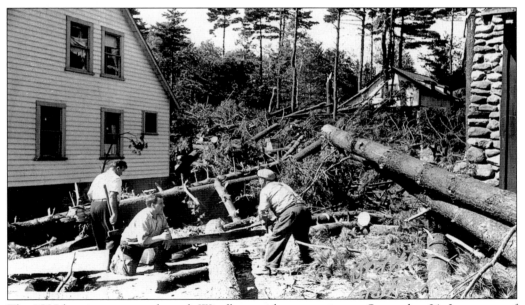

The 1938 hurricane swept through Windham without warning on September 21. It was one of the most destructive storms ever to hit New England. The great pine trees surrounding the lakes in Windham were laid low. In this photograph taken by Arthur Griffin, men using only handsaws begin the cleanup effort on West Shore Road.

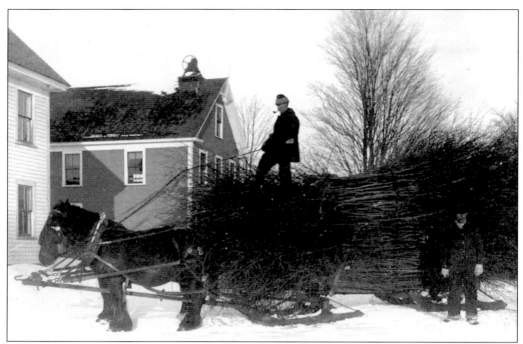

Clarence E. Harrington and Ernest Harrington deliver a load of witch hazel to the Gould witch hazel distillery on the turnpike. Both the Gould and Merrimack Witch Hazel Companies operated in Windham, creating one of the town's few industries. Carefully selected green twigs were boiled in huge vats and then mixed with alcohol.

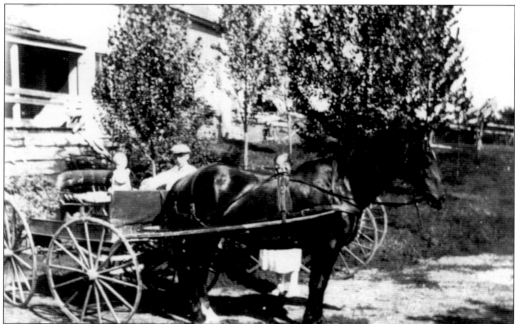

John H.K. Lamson is shown with his horse, wagon, and baby on his farm on the turnpike in Windham.

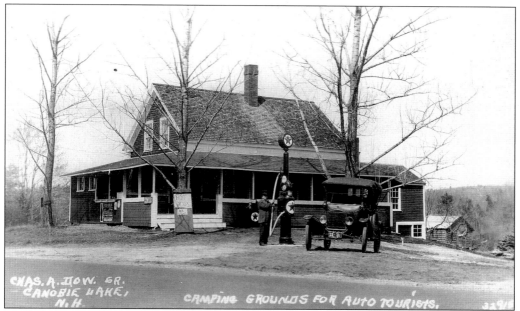

With the advent of the automobile, the old "Londonderry Turnpike" became Route 28, the direct route from Boston to the Lakes Region and the White Mountains. Many enterprising businessmen opened up shop along this roadway. Charles A. Dow owned this camping ground for automobile tourists on Seavey Pond. He also sold gas and other items from his store. The Londonderry Turnpike had been laid out in 1805, operated as a toll road, and ran from Concord, New Hampshire, to Boston.

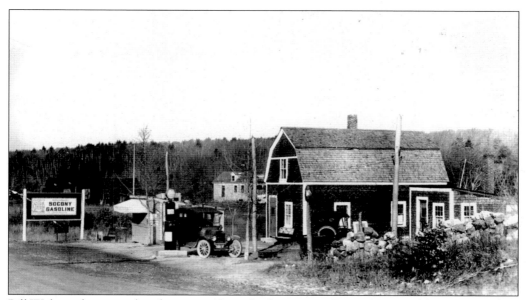

Bill Walters also catered to the tourists from this location on Route 28. He sold Socony gasoline that promised "Uniform Quality for Best Results." Laura's Ice Cream once operated here, offering penny cones. Here, as at Mason's Store, M.J. Sullivan's Furniture sponsored the bench.

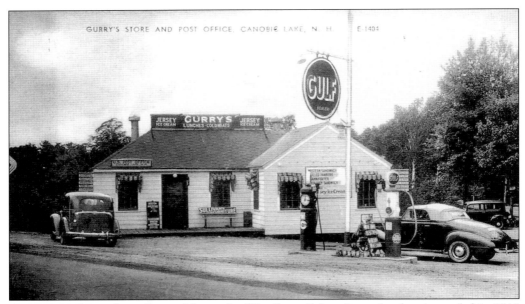

Gurry's was located on Route 28 on the Windham-Salem line. At the time of this 1943 photograph, the Canobie Lake Post Office had moved to this location. The vintage car waits to be gassed up at the pumps. The breakfast and lunch counter was a very popular spot with Windham folks, who could grab a bite to eat and also catch up with the local gossip. Sullivan Furniture is again sponsoring the bench.

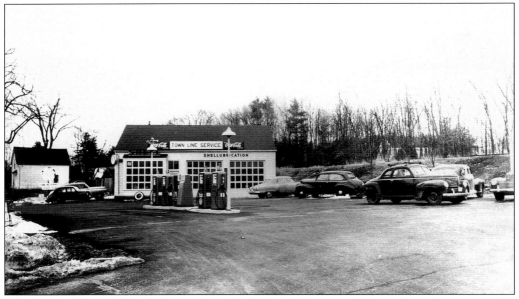

John Lamson Jr. and his father-in-law, Herb Partridge, opened Town Line Service on the Windham-Salem line. They ran the gas station and car-repair business for a number of years until George and Betty Rogers purchased the station in 1956. The Rogers family operated it until 2003, when it was closed so that Route 28 could be widened.

Seven

COBBETT'S POND

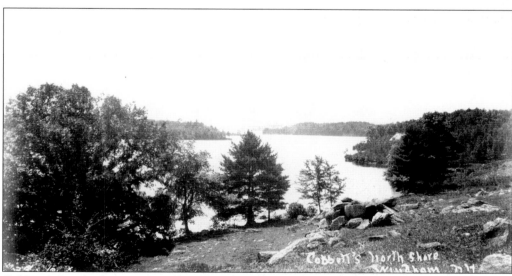

Cobbett's Pond takes its name from the Reverend Thomas Cobbet, a minister from Lynn and Ipswich, Massachusetts, who was granted 500 acres on the pond's north shore in 1662. The pond remained thereafter in its natural state, with nothing but woodlands and pastures along the shore, until Frank Ayer built the first cottage in 1886. The water of this spring-fed lake was clear and naturally soft, and the shoreline picturesque. Cobbett's Pond has been a beautiful backdrop to the memorable times that have centered on this special place. Lasting friendships have been made here, passionate romances pursued, and marriages celebrated. Parents have watched their children grow up here, to be followed by their children's children, one generation after another, celebrating life along these shores.

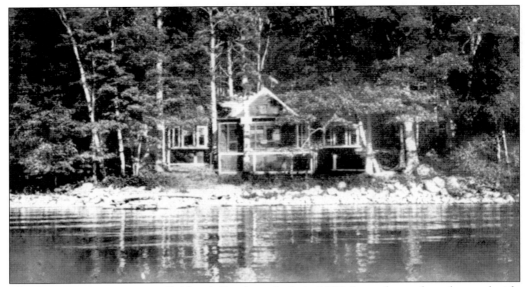

The first summer cottage on Cobbett's Pond was built in 1886. It was located on the south side of the narrows where Farmer Road is today. It had a beautiful view across a broad outlook to the sunset. The original cottage consisted of just what was under the center peak of the roof.

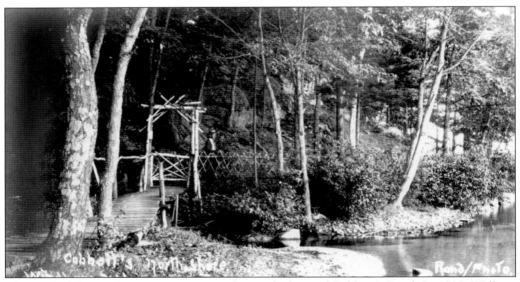

The land of the Harris Farm once ran to the north shore of Cobbett's Pond. In 1895, William Harris began developing his family's land into a summer cottage colony. We know from what he wrote in a newspaper column that he was an ardent environmentalist. In 1902, he called for the preservation of New Hampshire forestland. He also supported the protection of shorelines around lakes and ponds and called on the town to purchase open space decades before such notions became popular. He was a developer himself but strove to create a place that was in harmony with its natural setting. The north shore was an Arcadian paradise, as can be seen from this view of a rustic birch branch bridge built over Hollow Glen Brook.

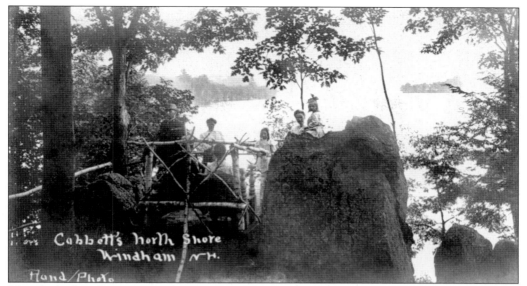

The Outlook at Fairview Rocks was one of the most picturesque spots on the entire shore of Cobbett's Pond and was a popular spot for church outings, Sunday school picnics, and even religious services. Birch railings adorn the perch that is set among the massive rocks on the north shore. This spot was later known as "the Crow's Nest."

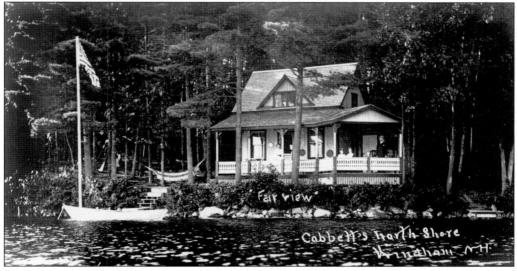

Harris was an unabashed promoter of the pond, stating, "If a quiet spot among the lakes and hills, and woods of the old Granite State is what you are looking for, in which to spend a summer vacation in a free and restful way, apart from the thronged resorts, and 'near to Nature's heart,' permit us to call your attention to Cobbett's Pond." William Brooks, the president of the Appalachian Mountain Club, was an early summer resident with his family. Fairview had a private setting and beautiful views. It rented for $6 a week or $20 a month in 1900.

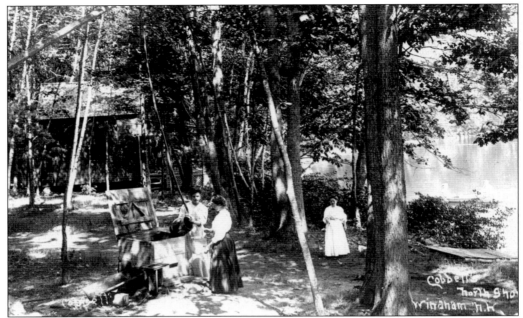

Summer residents draw water from the well on the north shore. Glenwood Cottage was built in 1895 and is pictured above. Harris's brochure read, "We intend to keep the North Shore a quiet family resort, and will rent only to persons furnishing satisfactory references." Oakwood, shown below, rented for $5 a week or $15 a month in 1900. The first water carnival on Cobbett's Pond was held on the north shore on August 12, 1910, at Partridge and Upham Cottages. There were swimming races, canoe races, and water sports. In the evening, decorated and illuminated canoes and boats made a beautiful pageant as they glided along the shore with fireworks above. Later, Japanese lanterns were lit and there was a costume parade.

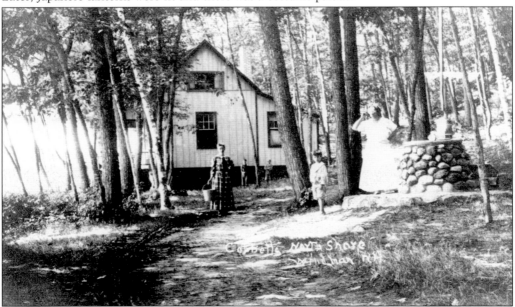

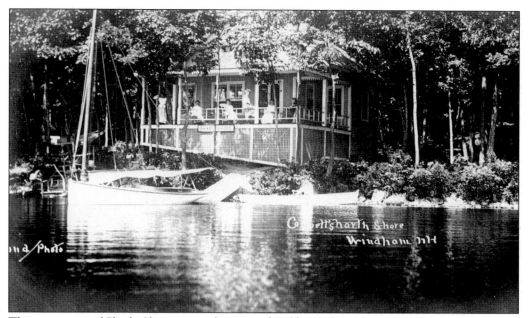

The occupants of Shady Shore enjoy the view of Cobbett's Pond from their front porch. Harris built this cottage in 1900. It was a superior dwelling with seven rooms, which rented for $8 a week or $30 a month. Harris provided the use of a good boat with each cottage rental.

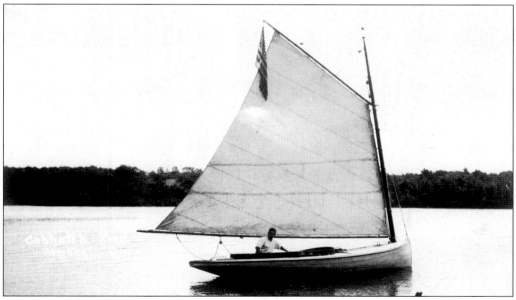

This beautiful sailboat catches a breeze in front of Shady Shore Cottage. Sailboats, rowboats, and canoes were the preferred forms of transportation on the water.

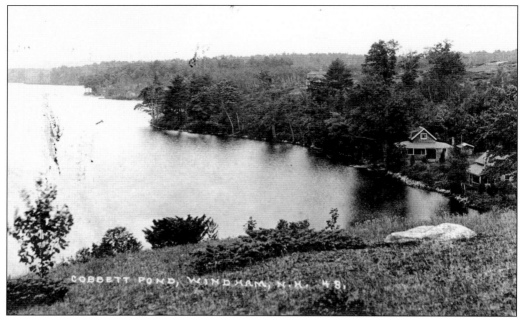

This photograph shows an early view of the head of the pond. George Dinsmore's cottages for summer vacationers can be seen at the right. Edward Searles owned this hill along with "the Rocky Pasture," which appears in the upper right. Searles's cottage can be seen through the trees.

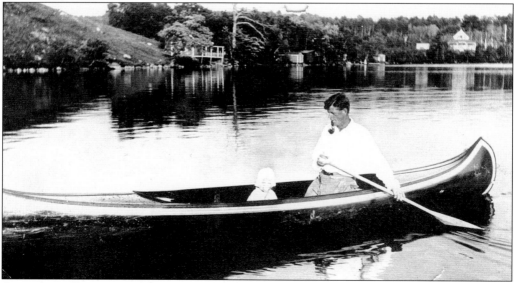

George Dinsmore Sr. and his young daughter Dorothy enjoy an early-morning canoe ride on the calm waters of Cobbett's Pond. The Methuen Cottage, at the bottom of the hill, was built in 1896, and next door was May's Cottage, constructed in 1897. Armstrong's shore is seen in the background, along with Pallister's Cottage, which was built in 1894. Dinsmore was a local legend known for his quick wit and tall tales. The photograph was taken c. 1917.

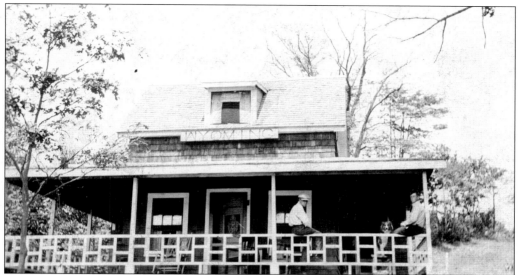

The Wyoming was George Dinsmore's cottage on Cobbett's Pond. He built it on the Rocky Pasture in 1911, the same year he married Edith Johnson, whom he met at Johnson's Boarding House. He moved to Wyoming with his new bride, and they lived in the wilds, first in only a tent and later in a small log cabin. They returned in 1913, and he moved this cottage down the ice after Edward Searles purchased the land it was built on. Both George and Edith Dinsmore were required to develop a certain proficiency with rifles and six-guns while living out West. They were known to display their prowess to bewildered onlookers. George Dinsmore is pictured on the porch at the right with his dog. The man at the left is unidentified.

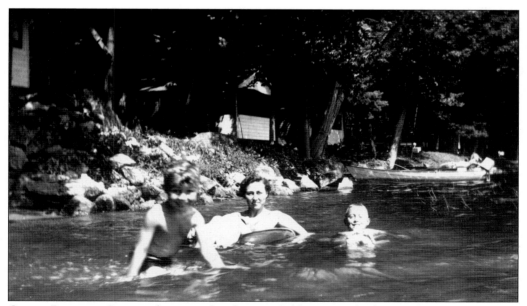

George Dinsmore Sr. rented tents on his shore at Cobbett's Pond. Shown relaxing in the water on a warm summer day in the 1940s are Ted Dooley (left), Ray Dooley (right), and their mother, Ruth.

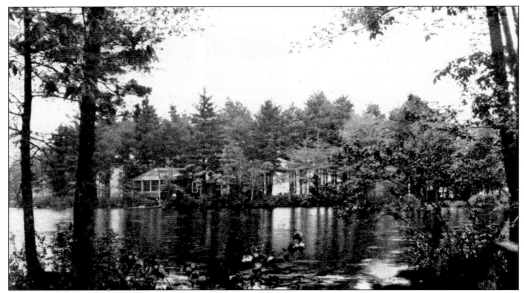

Johnson's Point is one of the landmarks on the lake. This narrow promontory, surrounded by water on three sides, was a place where the Johnson boarders could come and enjoy the lake. Later, the Johnsons had a large summer colony here where lots and cottages were leased for the summer. Maurice Armstrong and Lakeview Boarding House also leased tent lots on the shore.

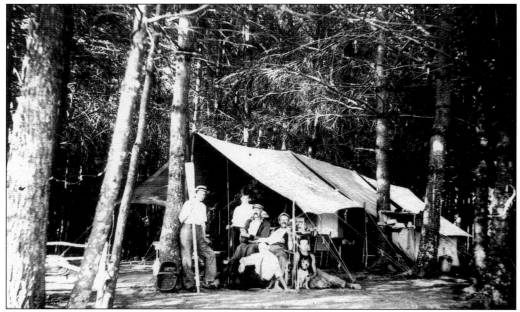

Arthur C. Sellon and his family were among the first people to rent a lot for tenting at Johnson's Point. Sellon is pictured fifth from the left (by the tent pole), and his son Arthur Sellon Jr. is second from the left (with the fishing pole). The others are unidentified. Arthur Sellon Jr. was the maternal grandfather of Richard McKinley, who still lives in the grove.

There has always been an unspoken rivalry between the campers on the lake and the townies. On September 17, 1922, a match was held between the Windham Town Team and the Cobbett's Pond Athletic Club. The baseball game was held as planned, and the Cobbett's Pond team won 9-4. The photograph shows Roy LeFavour and Alva Perkins of the Cobbett's Pond Athletic Club in front of the cottage their family rented for the summer on Johnson's Point.

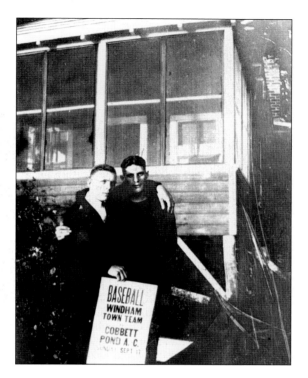

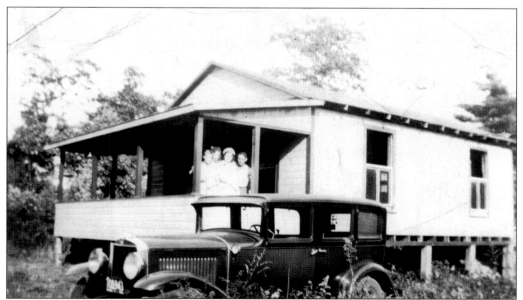

In 1929, some 60 acres of land off Ministerial Road was divided into 975 lots with a beach and playground. The waterfront lots were $50, and the back lots were $20. The Great Depression hit, and the lots were slow to sell. The developers began a promotional deal in the Malden-Medford area where grocery stores redeemed coupons for a lot after a set amount of coffee, tea, or canned goods was bought. Gerrish Littlefield's cottage (seen here) was built on a lot at Community Beach in October 1930, after he redeemed Hatchet brand coupons in Malden.

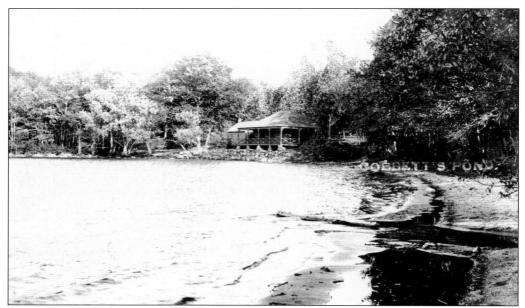

The Richardson brothers were the first to entertain picnickers and fishermen at the lower end of Cobbett's Pond. "Long Albert" Simpson purchased their property in 1888. He opened Sycamore Grove, which became an immediate success. A pavilion with dining facilities was built, boats were available for rent, and a natural, sandy beach allowed for swimming. The popularity of the grove increased after Julia Baker purchased the property in the early 1900s. The pavilion also hosted local events, like a Woman's Club concert in 1913, which witnessed many of the guests arriving in boats and canoes decorated with Japanese lanterns.

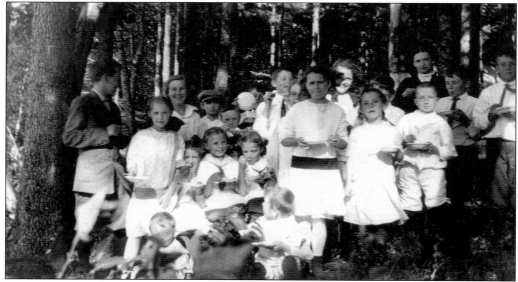

Children at a picnic at Baker's in 1911 eat ice cream out of china bowls.

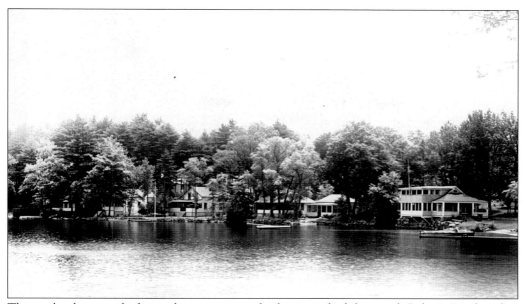

This early photograph shows the cottages at the lower end of the pond. Baker's Pavilion has been enlarged, and the addition cantilevers out over the water. A beautiful, wooded speedboat can be seen at the dock.

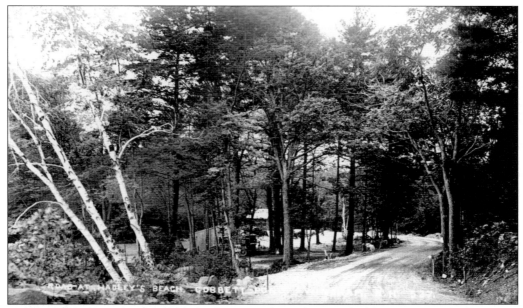

Cobbett's Pond Road passes near Hadley's Beach in this wonderful scene. During the 1930s, Julia Baker subdivided her grove and sold a section of the beach to Tom Hadley of Lawrence, Massachusetts. Hadley opened another bathing resort. The refreshment stand and an old car can be seen behind the trees.

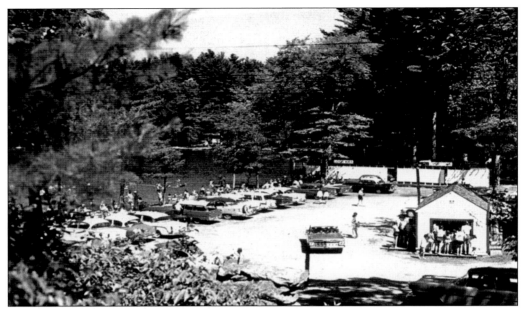

At one time, there were five beaches operating on Cobbett's Pond: Dunkan's, Armstrong's, Bella Vista, Hadley's, and Sandy. The beaches prospered from the 1930s through the 1970s, with Dunkan's closing last in the 1980s. Changing tastes, increasing affluence, backyard pools, and a changing customer profile all led to their demise. This picture shows Hadley's in the 1950s. You may recognize it now as the Windham town beach.

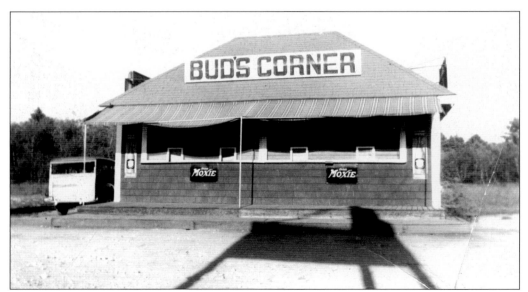

Bud's Corner was a local institution and gathering place, especially for the older kids from Windham and Cobbett's Pond. It was within walking distance of Pine Terrace and Community Beach. Many friendships were made here while enjoying fried clams, a burger, or an ice-cream cone. The stand was located across from the cemetery where Rogers Field is today. Bud and Mildred Travis operated the stand for many years until 1974.

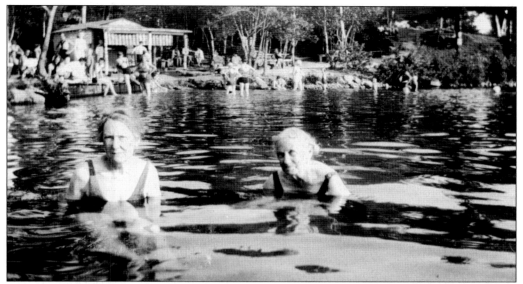

Maurice Armstrong opened Armstrong's Beach in 1932. In this early photograph, the concession stand is seen with its rustic front porch held up by birch posts. A beautiful pine grove was perfect for picnics, and a natural sandy beach for swimming. The shoreline itself, however, was quite rocky. Two unidentified ladies enjoy the water.

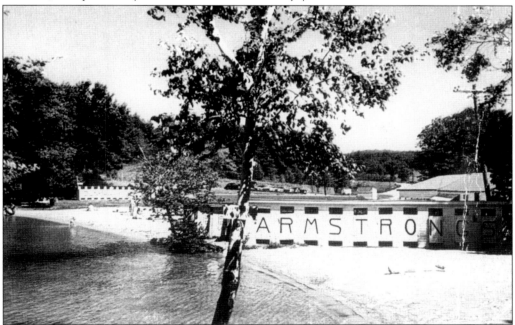

Armstrong's and Dunkan's Beaches sat side by side, with a small brook separating the two properties. George Dunkley opened Dunkan's Beach in the 1930s, and it became a very successful, lucrative business. Dunkley built a large pavilion with a snack bar, bowling alleys, and pinball machines. He rented a slew of little black and white rowboats. A 1950 advertisement for Dunkan's Beach offered boating, bathing, speedboat rides, and parking for 1,000 cars.

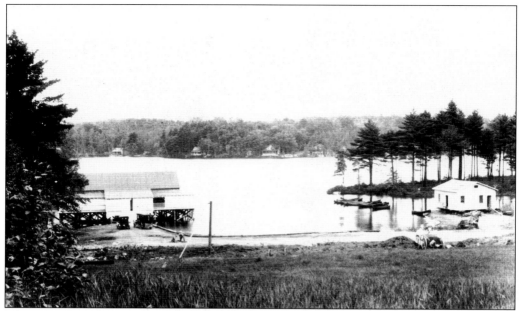

John Evans saw the popularity of Baker's Grove and decided to open a competing business. He purchased the Bella Vista Farm in 1923 and set about making improvements. A pleasant beach was created out of what was once a marsh. In 1925, he built a dance hall out over the lake. All the major orchestras of the day came to play here, and the sound of the big bands could be heard drifting across the water as up to 500 people danced inside. The dance hall burned in 1931.

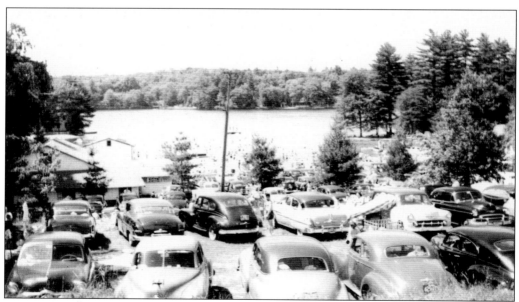

Bella Vista Beach is shown here in the 1950s. The building that once housed the speakeasy Club Mariana during Prohibition can be seen near the water. Charlie and Avis Thwaites bought the beach in 1947, and it remained in their family into the 1980s. The beach was very popular as the favorite hangout of teenagers in the 1950s and 1960s.

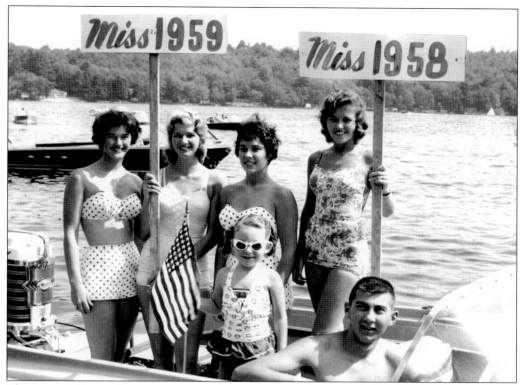

The Miss Cobbett's Pond contest was the big event in the area. Pictured here are, from left to right, Polly Ann Sanborn, Carol Drowns (Miss 1959), Carol Androwski, Ronnie Lou Thwaites (in the sunglasses), Marie Chadwick (Miss 1958), and Al Tomaselli.

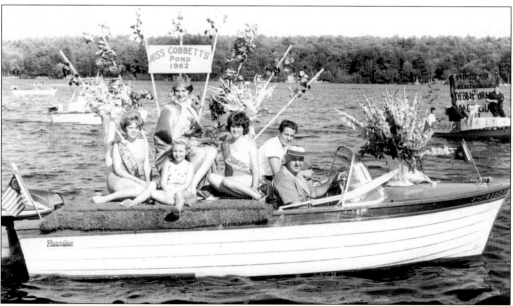

Miss Cobbett's Pond contestants ride in the boat parade during the summer of 1962.

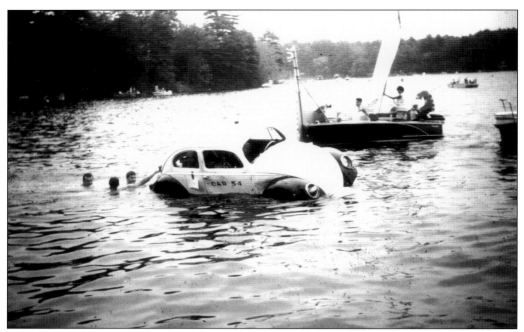

The residents of Cobbett's Pond decorated their boats extravagantly for the annual boat parade. Dot West has chronicled this event with photographs from 1957 through 1968 that show some of the amazing entries. The parade was also the time for the newly crowned Miss Cobbett's Pond to be introduced to the residents of the lake. A floating Volkswagen bug (above) was entered as "Car 54" in one parade, and a Mississippi steamboat (below) appeared in another.

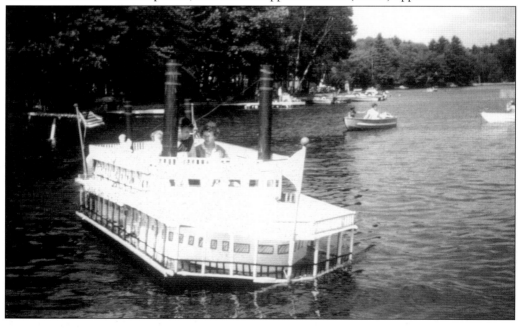

Eight
SEARLES CASTLE

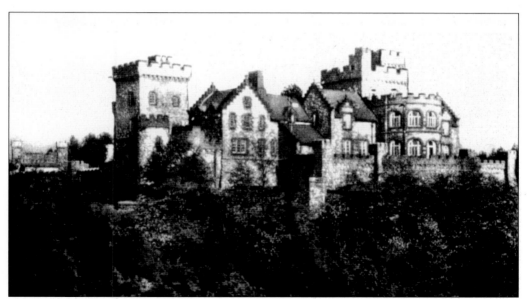

Searles Castle is one of Windham's most prominent landmarks. In 1902, Edward Francis Searles began acquiring land in Windham. He eventually owned more than 1,300 acres that ran from Jenny's Hill to Dinsmore's Hill, then down to the shores of Canobie Lake and Cobbett's Pond. It was a magnificent setting with panoramic views in all directions and the perfect place for Searles to build a replica of an English castle. Construction started in 1905 and was completed in 1912. The castle was a magnificent example of authentic Tudor and medieval architecture.

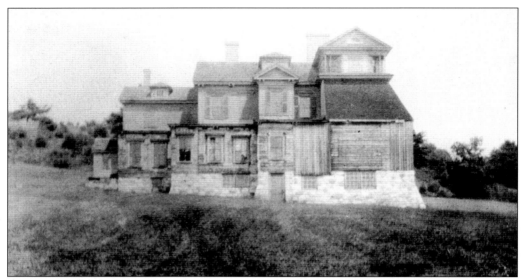

In 1904, Searles began making improvements to his estate. William Harris reported, "Edward F. Searles, the Methuen millionaire, is making great improvements on his estate at Jenny's Hill. The large mansion house has been moved back a considerable distance to higher site, commanding a grand prospect, and additions and alterations are being made." Searles also built an observation tower nearby. The mansion house is shown above, after it was abandoned.

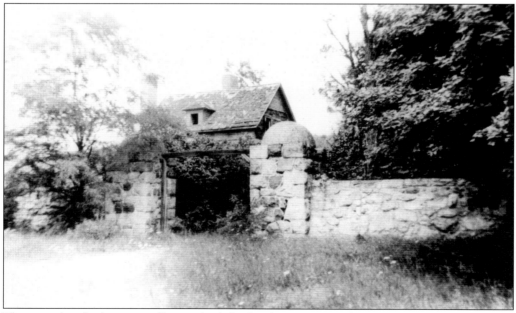

These six-foot-high stone walls were built by Searles in 1904 at the entrance to his estate at the corner of County and Governor Dinsmoor Roads. When Stanton-Harcourt was built, he abandoned this site on Jenny's Hill in favor of the more convenient Dinsmoor's Hill location. Known as the Preist Place, this farm was beautifully remodeled by Searles but was later just left to rot.

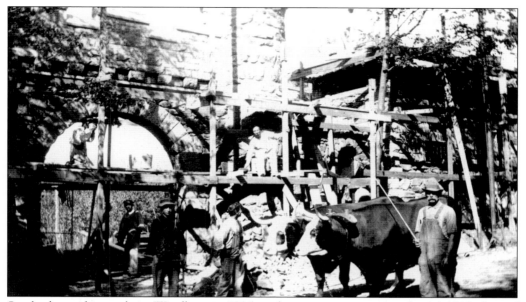

Searles began his castle in Windham in 1905, and construction continued until 1912. One of his largest projects was enclosing his estate with massive stone walls. A special quarry was opened to supply the granite. In this photograph, stonemasons build the massive arch for the gates and the adjoining gatehouse. (Courtesy of Nesmith Library.)

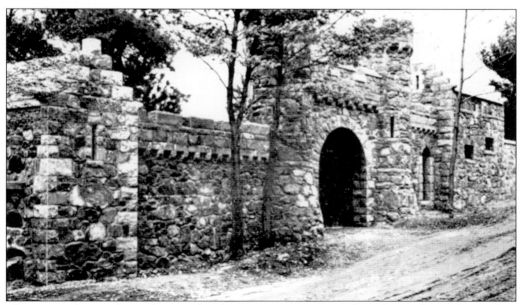

This postcard view shows the completed main entrance gate and gatehouse, located on Indian Rock Road. This was a focal point of the estate to outsiders until Indian Rock Road (Route 111) was relocated in the 1950s. Sadly, this beautiful turreted gate with its magnificent stonework fell into disrepair and was torn down in the 1980s.

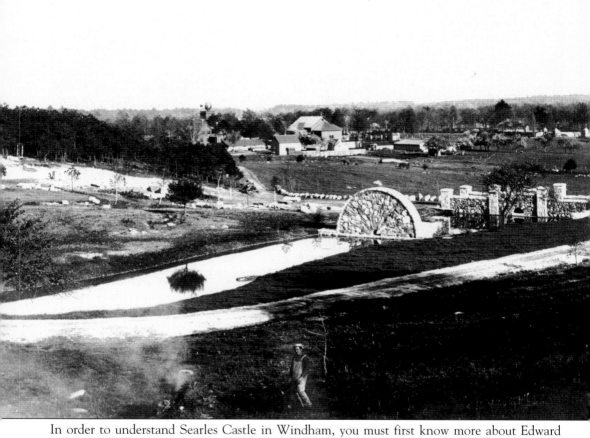

In order to understand Searles Castle in Windham, you must first know more about Edward Francis Searles. His personal motto was "They say. What say they? Let them say." He was born on July 4, 1841, on a farm in Methuen, Massachusetts, that would eventually become his Pine Lodge estate. As a young man, he worked in a Methuen cotton mill to support his widowed mother. An early love affair ended tragically when Catherine Linehan jilted him for his brother Andrew. Searles eventually moved to New York, where he became a very successful interior designer with Herter Brothers, whose client list included the who's who of the gilded age. Through his work with Herter Brothers, he met Mary Hopkins, reportedly the richest widow in America, in 1880. Searles was 40 when he met the 62-year-old woman. Her husband, Mark, had been a partner in the Central Pacific Railroad. Searles's and Hopkins's working relationship turned into something more, and in 1887, they were married in Trinity Cathedral in New York City. Was Searles a fortune hunter? No one will ever know for sure, but Mary, who was a spiritualist, said she saw in Searles a "kindred spirit." Prior to her death in 1891, Mary voided her prenuptial agreement and changed her will, leaving the bulk of her vast wealth to her husband. Edward Searles soon set about indulging his fantasies with Mary's $30 million. In Windham, he created a medieval fantasy world, with an English castle, bridges, arches, ponds stocked with fish, barns, and lodges. It was a place where the eccentric Searles could be lord of the manor. Edward Frances Searles died in 1920. He left his personal secretary, Arthur Walker, Stanton-Harcourt in Windham and $50 million. Walker died in the castle in 1928.

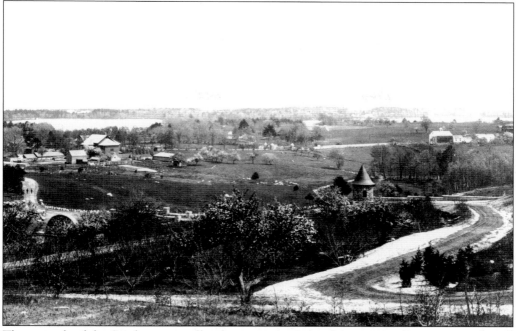

The grounds of the Searles estate offered panoramic views of the surrounding countryside and of Canobie Lake. Three miles of roadway wound throughout the estate. Edward Searles was not well loved by the many in Windham who felt he was buying up the whole town and making it his private domain. One person who refused all the lucrative offers to sell out was Dan Roy, whose farm can be seen to the right.

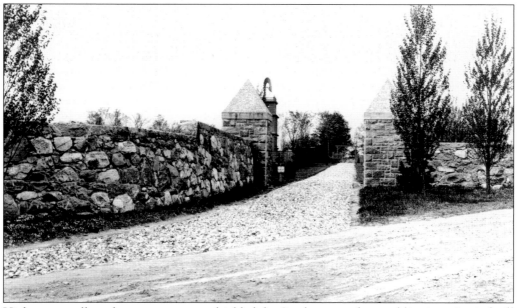

High stone walls and an entrance gate shielded the Searles estate from public view. A windmill can be seen atop the tower at Morrison Lodge. This wall enclosed the No. 1 Schoolhouse after 1909.

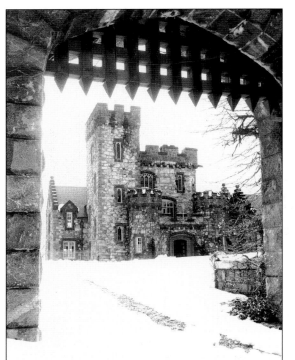

The castle in Windham is a one-quarter-scale replica of Stanton-Harcourt castle in Lincoln, England, to whose ancient owners Searles had traced his ancestry. Architect Henry Vaughn was sent to England to draw reconstructed plans from the ruins. The Stanton-Harcourt castle's coat of arms became the official emblem for this castle. The castle is constructed of native fieldstone and trimmed with cut granite and dark red sandstone. Fine craftsman were brought over from Europe to work on its construction. Attention to detail is noted in the battlement towers, turrets, bastions, and walls, which are eight feet thick. Searles's love of art was manifest in the richly carved woodwork, paneled walls, hand-hewn timbered ceilings, and beautiful fireplaces.

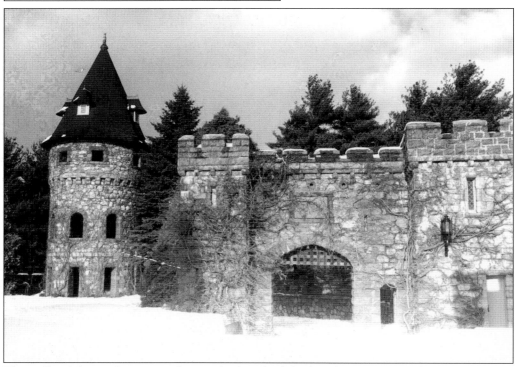

The walls of the castle courtyard are eight feet thick at their base. Two guard towers flank the traditional portcullis gate. The round clock tower contained Westminster chimes.

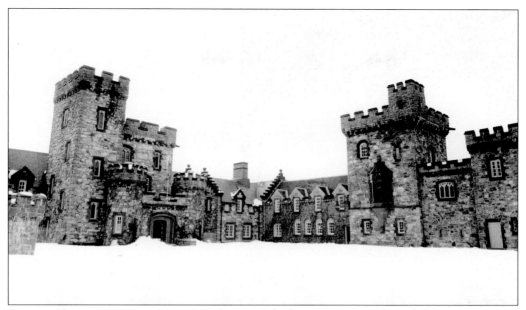

Stanton-Harcourt contains 20 principal rooms. The largest tower, at the right, contains a spiral staircase leading to guest quarters. Originally, the space between the tower and the main building was unfinished. Searles never completed construction on the castle. The estate itself was surrounded by walls on only three sides; the rest was enclosed with wire fencing.

The main reception hall contains the famous doors from Windsor Castle in Berkshire, England. The floors are tiled, the walls richly paneled, and the ceiling timbered. The grand staircase features magnificent woodcarving created by master craftsmen. The doors open into the living room. Two sunrooms beyond the living room are highlighted with curved walls of leaded-glass windows offering spectacular views.

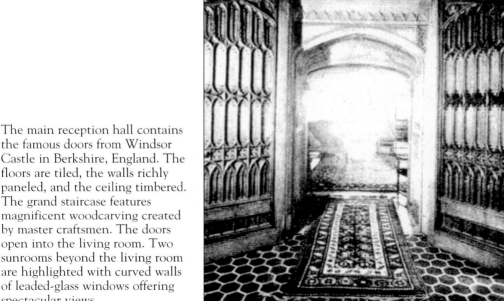

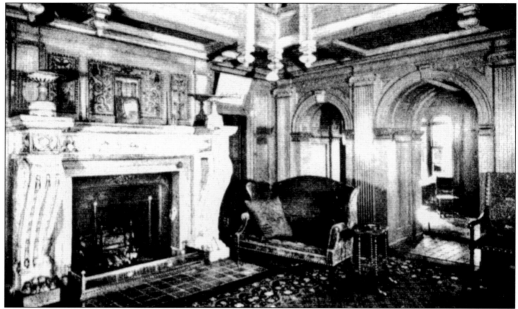

The marble fireplace in the living room is inlaid with gold and was taken from Napoleon's favorite room in the Tuileries Grand Palace in Paris. While considered a priceless artifact, it cost Searles $50,000. The living room features carved-oak paneling and opens to a balcony above.

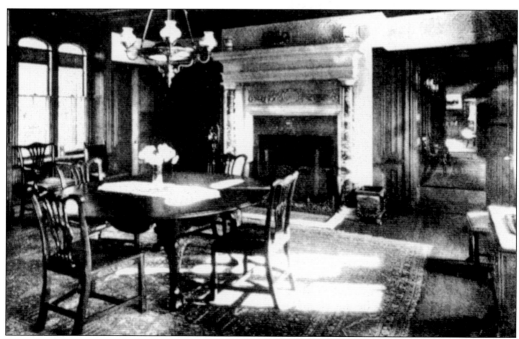

The dining room includes a fireplace mantle that was aboard a ship that sank in New York harbor. The salt water turned the marble beautiful hues of blue and green.

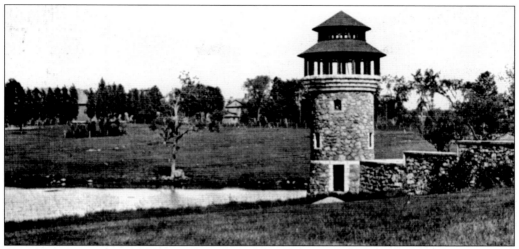

Searles Tower stands guard over the ponds and pastures of the beautiful estate. Morrison Lodge can be seen at the center of the photograph. According to longtime residents of Windham, Searles chose to live at Morrison Lodge rather than at Stanton-Harcourt. Searles became a citizen of Windham in 1913 but left after the selectmen tried to take advantage of the potential tax windfall that his vast wealth presented. In 1914, he took up residency in New York.

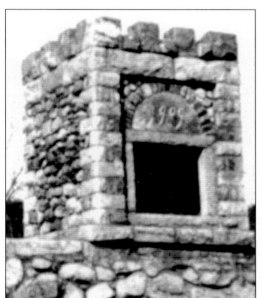

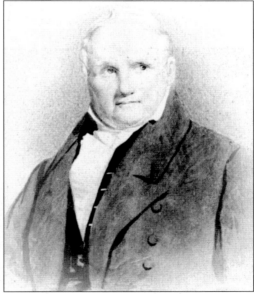

Gov. Samuel Dinsmoor was born in Windham on July 1, 1766, growing up on the family farm on Jenny's Hill. He prepared for college with Parson Williams at his academy in Windham and graduated from Dartmouth in 1789. Settling in Keene, New Hampshire, Dinsmoor was elected to Congress in 1811. In 1831, he was elected governor and held office for three consecutive terms. William C. Harris suggested that a monument be built to mark the governor's birthplace. Edward Searles, the owner of Dinsmoor farm, agreed to pay to have a monument erected. On July 9, 1909, more than 200 dignitaries, including Gov. Henry Quimby, attended the unveiling ceremonies. The governor was conveyed from the train station in the automobile of William F. Meserve.

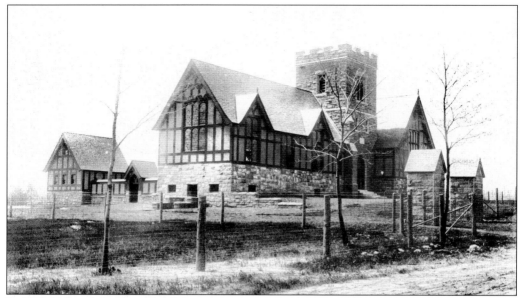

In 1907, Edward Searles offered the town a new school if it would agree to just two requests. He wanted ownership of the old No. 1 Schoolhouse and he wanted to relocate Range Road to give his estate more privacy. The town agreed, and Searles School was built at a cost of more than $40,000. Noted architect Henry Vaughn designed it. The school is shown just after its opening. Searles's wire fencing surrounds the property.

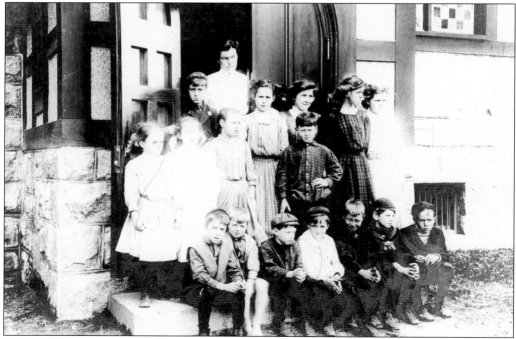

Students at Searles School in 1911 include Mabel Webster, Margaret Griffin, Bertha Lamson, Mildred Johnson, Cora Kelly, Leon Gould, Elmer Cutting, John Lamson, Charlie Sanborn, Ethel Gould, Albert Gould, Frank ?, and Alfred ?.

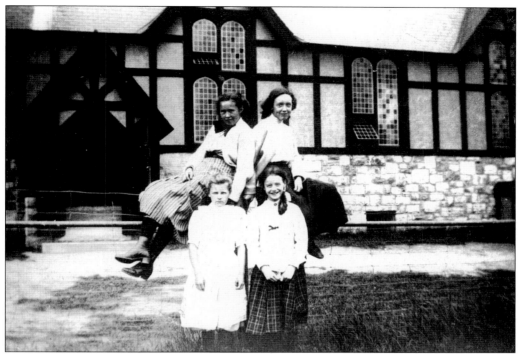

One of the first graduating classes was still nostalgic for its old school. In "The Class Hymn," Bertha Lamson wrote, "Our childhood days were spent within, The brick school house 'neath the hill, And tho' its wall are ours no more—It lives in memory still."

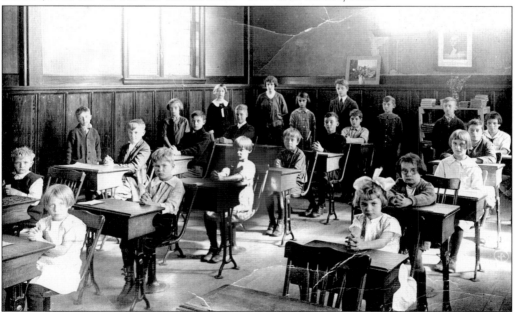

A class of schoolchildren is presided over by Emma Cashion. The sunlight streams into the classroom through stained-glass windows. Everything is in order with all hands folded on the desks.

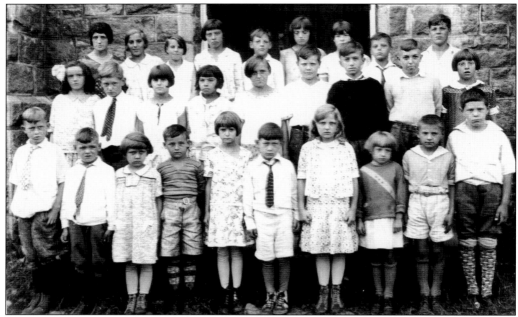

Emma Cashion is shown with a group of students from the 1930s. She taught here for more than 25 years and was an institution at the school. In the beginning of her career, this dedicated teacher taught all eight grades in one room.

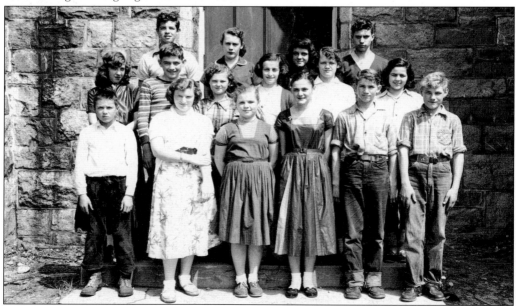

At the time of this photograph in 1953, grades seven and eight were taught at Searles School. Pictured here are, from left to right, the following members of the eighth-grade class: (front row) James Chadwick, Daryl Butterfield, Gail Sturtevent, Carol Zins, Bob Albright, and Norman Bone; (middle row) Ramona Edwards, Austin Crowe, Edith Frenette, Janice Dean, Doris Ackerman, and Suzanne Landry; (back row) Wilfred Johnson, Sandra Lannan, Patsy McLennan, and Richard Beauregard.

Nine
THE WINDHAM PLAYHOUSE

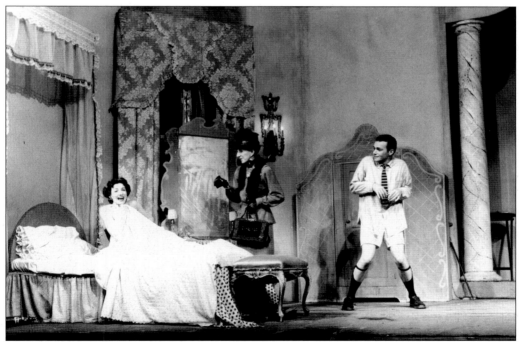

In the summer of 1946, the glamour and spectacle of a great summer theater burst onto the scene in the small town of Windham. Everett Austin Jr., better known as "Chick," converted an old barn into a theater on the Lt. Joseph Smith farm. Austin was the director of the Ringling Museum of Art in Sarasota, Florida. The playhouse became an instant success, and many nights, patrons had to be turned away at the door. Pictured here is a scene from *Room Service*, which was staged in 1951. (Courtesy of Wadsworth Atheneum.)

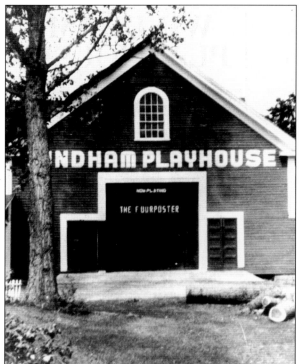

The original barn from which the playhouse was constructed was built in the 1830s. The section housing the lobby and restrooms had been added in the 1920s. The proscenium opening was the back wall of the barn, and the stage that was added was unusually large for a summer theater: 50 feet wide by 24 feet deep. The proscenium opening was 28 feet. The grid was 30 feet above the stage, enabling the stagehands to "fly" the scenery—that is, to lift it up out of the way. The solid pine beams holding up the stage had been salvaged from an old railroad trestle. The theater sat 300 patrons. Its unique box seats were brightly enameled sleighs from the 1880s and had come from Laura Austin's estate up the road. The lobby decorations were costume designs from Austin's previous productions. (Courtesy of Wadsworth Atheneum.)

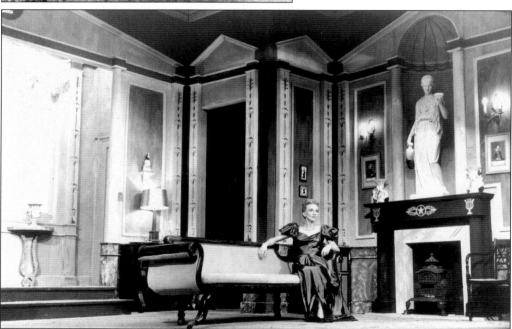

The stage sets were simply breathtaking because of the attention to detail Chick Austin demanded. The stage was filled with antiques and fine art either purchased locally or borrowed from his mother's home. This scene is from the 1948 production of *Laura*. The architectural details and classical statue are extraordinary. (Courtesy of Wadsworth Atheneum.)

Shown here is the top half of a broadside announcing a production at the Windham Playhouse during its first season in 1946. Everett Austin is presenting *Ten Nights in a Bar Room*, a drama in five acts. It is to be a "spectacle extraordinary." The broadside notes, "The scenery used in to-night's production was painted originally for The Old Haddam Opera House on the Connecticut River. It was constructed in 1870 and is one of the few surviving examples of American Stagecraft of the period."

WINDHAM PLAYHOUSE
WINDHAM, N. H.

SPECTACLE EXTRAORDINARY!

AUGUST 13. 14. 15. 16. 17. 1946

MR. EVERETT AUSTIN
PRESENTS

"TEN NIGHTS IN A BAR-ROOM"

A DRAMA IN FIVE ACTS

Dramatized from T. S. Arthur's Novel of the same name, by the late
WILLIAM W. PRATT

Entire Production Under the Supervision of
MISS ELIZABETH M. KIMBALL

The scenery used in to-night's production was painted originally for The Old Haddam Opera House on the Connecticut River. It was constructed in 1870 and is one of the few surviving examples of American Stagecraft of the period.

Additional Spectacular Effects by Mr. James Hellyar
See Other Side For Important Announcement

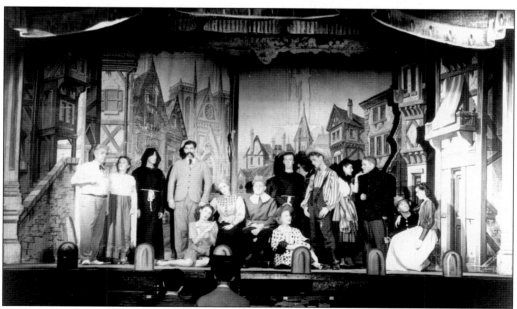

This scene is either from *Ten Nights in a Bar Room* (in 1946) or *The Drunkard* (staged in 1947). The scenery from the Old Haddam Opera House was used in both plays. *The Drunkard* was written by William Smith in 1844 and was a famous temperance melodrama, a piece of Americana made famous by P.T. Barnum. (Courtesy of Wadsworth Atheneum.)

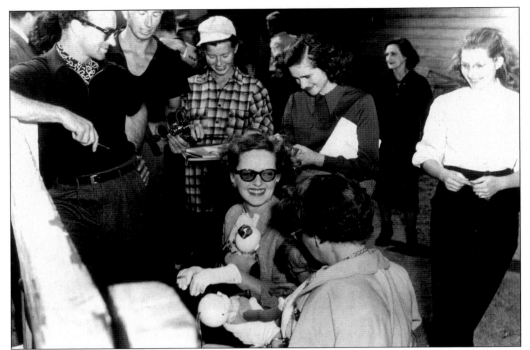

In 1948, Bette Davis agreed to attend one of Austin's performances at the Windham Playhouse. Although Austin was a celebrity himself in the art world, he was star-struck by this Hollywood actress. She is shown chatting with fans and signing autographs in front of the playhouse, after the performance of *Voice of the Turtle*. (Courtesy of Wadsworth Atheneum.)

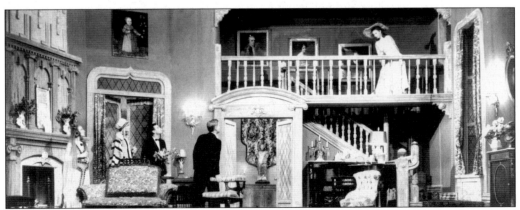

In this scene from *Rebecca*, staged in September 1947, Chick Austin performs the role of Maxim de Winter. Laura Austin's portrait collection is seen hanging on the walls. Some of the now-famous actors who performed on stage at the playhouse include Rod Steiger, Lee Marvin, and Richard Deacon. (Courtesy of Wadsworth Atheneum.)

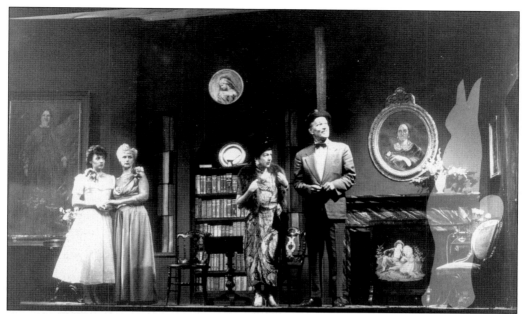

In 1954, the Pulitzer Prize–winning comedy *Harvey* was presented at the Windham Playhouse. It starred Moyna Macgill as Veta Louise Simmons. In her third season at the playhouse, Macgill was a well-known actress on both the English and American stages. Her daughter was the film and television star Angela Lansbury, and her son Edgar Lansbury was a set designer at the playhouse. (Courtesy of Wadsworth Atheneum.)

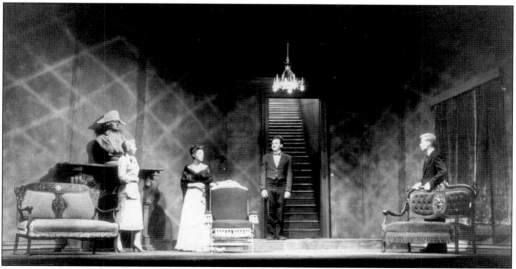

No Exit, a work by Jean Paul Sartre, was the closing production at the playhouse in 1949. The playbill reads, "We believe this play is Sartre at his most violent and most theatrical pitch. . . . Two brilliant young actresses, Miss Marion Winters and Miss Genevieve Griffin, have been especially engaged for this production." (Courtesy of Wadsworth Atheneum.)

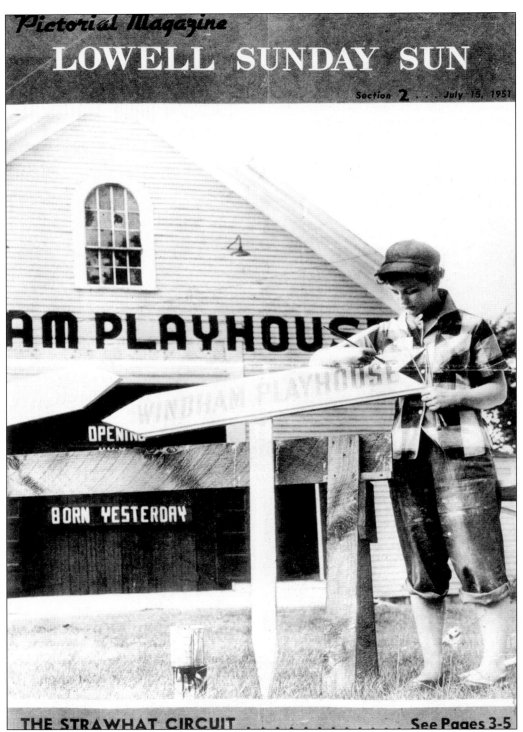

AM PLAYHOUSE

WINDHAM PLAYHOUSE

OPENING

BORN YESTERDAY

THE STRAWHAT CIRCUIT . . . . See Pages 3-5

The Windham Playhouse was featured on the cover of the magazine section of the *Lowell Sun* on July 15, 1951. *Born Yesterday* was set to open. (Courtesy of Wadsworth Atheneum.)

Chick Austin was a talented and successful art director at both the Wadsworth Atheneum and the Ringling Museum, but his passion was always the theater. Soon after his arrival at both Hartford and Sarasota, a theater became an integral part of the museums. Austin is pictured on a playbill for *Born Yesterday*. One playbill notes the producer's biography as follows:

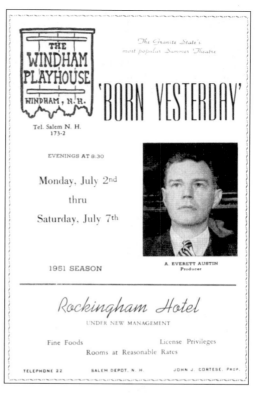

Everett Austin, owner and producer of the Windham Playhouse has long been active in the theater as actor, producer and scene designer on the East and West coasts and in Florida where he is the director of the Ringling Museum of Art in Sarasota. Outstanding among his productions are "Maya" at the Gate Theatre, Hollywood, and "Tis Pity" in Hartford, where he won critical acclaim for his interpretation of the Prince in his production of "Hamlet." Windham players will remember Austin in leading roles in "Angel Street" and "Blythe Spirit" of the previous season. Last winter he appeared with the Sarasota Players in "Rebecca" and other plays.

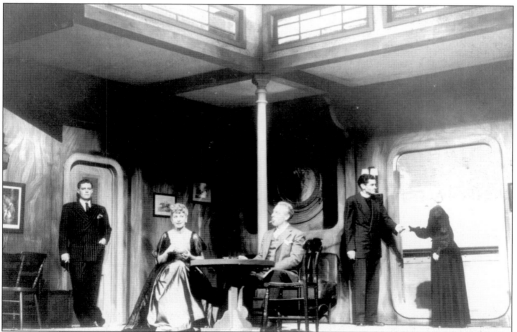

Shown here is a scene from *Outward Bound*, presented in the 1948 season. Austin stands at the left. (Courtesy of Wadsworth Atheneum.)

125

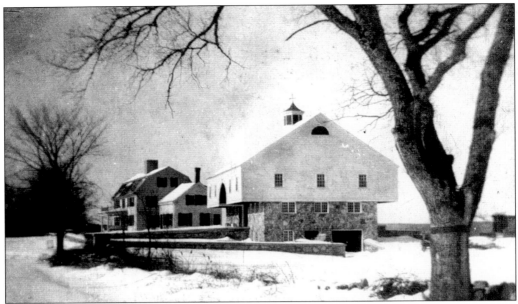

Capt. John Cristy built this beautiful Colonial (above) *c.* 1746. The house sits on the brow of a hill and once offered a beautiful view of Cobbett's Pond. Laura Austin was a wealthy Boston matron who purchased the Senter farm in 1913 and then set about making various improvements. She later purchased the Joseph Smith farm further up Range Road. At this country retreat, she and her son Everett could get away from city life in Boston. The barn next door was remodeled into a house reminiscent of the architecture found in the Pennsylvania countryside, where she had grown up as a child. She named it Barn Manor. Laura later gave the Joseph Smith farm to her son as a wedding present. Chick loved this sanctuary in Windham. When the playhouse was in operation, he held court at Barn Manor with the principal actors, while others stayed next door or at a cottage on Cobbett's Pond. The house is pictured below after extensive remodeling.

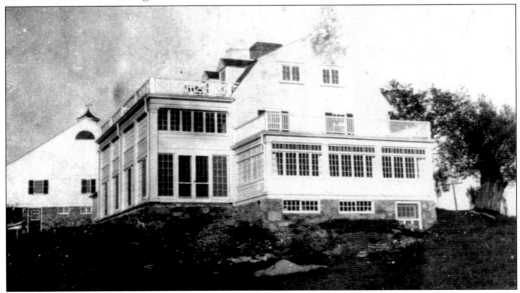

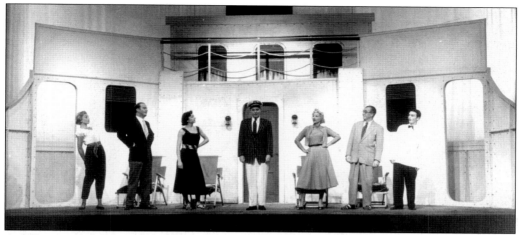

A different playbill biography of Austin states the following:

Many people love theatre; Mr. Austin loves good theater, and here at the Windham Playhouse he puts his belief in the power of the production as a whole. Settings must be right, they must also have what he calls "flair." The plays must have varied appeal; each should be a New York success, and more than not written by a top-ranking playwright. [One must have] an acting company in which each player works to make the play as a whole the real star of the piece.

Clutterbuck was staged during the 1953 season of the Windham Playhouse. Austin stands at the center. (Courtesy of Wadsworth Atheneum.)

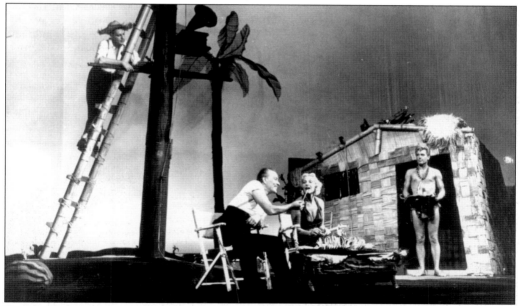

Beatrice Ganz stars as Susan in the comedy *Little Hut*, performed during the 1954 season at the Windham Playhouse. Austin cast his devoted, longtime friend in many productions over the years. "A favorite with audiences, loved for herself and respected for her work by fellow actors in past and present seasons, she will be remembered for many brilliant and exciting performances." (Courtesy of Wadsworth Atheneum.)

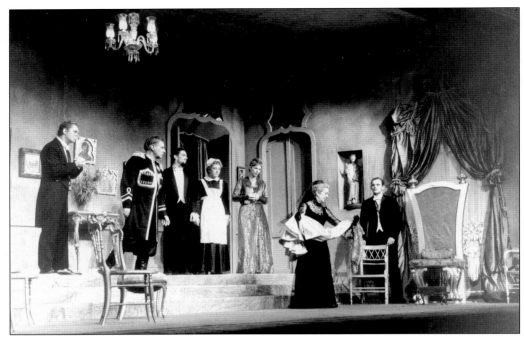

Anastasia was staged at the Windham Playhouse in 1956. Austin is shown playing the role of Prince Bounine. A story told by Lynn McMurrey, a young actor, illustrates how the dedication and hard work of the cast and crew, which included residents Herb and Rose Crucius, contributed to the success of the theater. In the summer of 1952, Hurricane Carol hit, causing severe damage. The electricity was knocked out, but the show went on as scheduled in front of a full house, by candlelight. (Courtesy of Wadsworth Atheneum.)

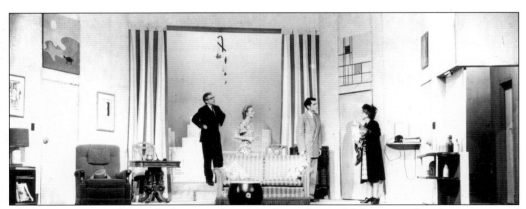

The magic, spectacle, and glamour that transformed an old barn in the sleepy town of Windham into one of America's premier summer theaters came to and end in 1957. Chick Austin, the magician who cast his spell on everyone and led the company of actors that put on so many memorable productions here in Windham, died at age 56. He was buried next to the playhouse, in the Cemetery on the Hill. In the play shown here, Austin appears in a production with a modern set in the mid-1950s. (Courtesy of Wadsworth Atheneum.)